Beyond These Walls

INNOVATORS IN MINISTRY

Beyond These Walls

Building the Church in a Built-Out Neighborhood

RICHARD L. DUNAGIN
WITH LYLE E. SCHALLER

INNOVATORS IN MINISTRY

ABINGDON PRESS
Nashville

BEYOND THESE WALLS:
BUILDING THE CHURCH IN A BUILT-OUT NEIGHBORHOOD

Copyright © 1999 by Abingdon Press

This book is printed on acid-free paper.

Library of Congress Cataloging-in-Publication Data

Dunagin, Richard L.
    Beyond these walls : building the church in a built-out neighborhood / Richard L. Dunagin with Lyle E. Schaller.
        p.   cm.—(Innovators in ministry)
    Includes bibliographical references.
    ISBN 0-687-08596-9 (pbk. : alk. paper)
    1. Church growth.   2. City churches—Texas—Dallas—Case studies.
3. Church growth—Methodist Church—Case studies.   4. Lake Highlands United Methodist Church (Dallas, Tex.)   I. Schaller, Lyle E.
II. Title.   III. Series.
BV652.25.D86   1999   98-46440
                                                                              CIP

Scripture quotations are from the New Revised Standard Version Bible, copyright © 1989, by the Division of Christian Education of the National Council of the Churches of Christ in the United States of America.

99 00 01 02 03 04 05 06 07 08 — 10 9 8 7 6 5 4 3 2 1

MANUFACTURED IN THE UNITED STATES OF AMERICA

*To the disciples of Jesus Christ
at Lake Highlands United Methodist Church.
They are the true heroes of the turnaround
that has occurred in our midst.
It is only because of their faithfulness
that the church is advancing
into the twenty-first century
as a strong and viable force for God,
and I appreciate them all.*

CONTENTS

ACKNOWLEDGMENTS

Whenever I complete any project as large as this, I realize how indebted I am to God for the countless family and friends who have aided my journey. God has richly blessed my life with caring and insightful people who have given me far more than I have returned. Theresa has served as my devoted wife and friend for more than half of our lives, and together we have been privileged to participate in the development of Shelah, Rachel, and Renée, our incredible daughters. The love of a great family is one of God's choicest gifts.

I am grateful for the laity of the churches in which I have served over the years. From them I have learned a great deal. Together we formed a partnership to develop as fully as we could the ministries that God assigned us. Every congregation I have served has been remarkably open to change. Perhaps surprisingly, no one has ever seriously quoted to me the Seven Last Words of the Church: "We never did it that way before." Lake Highlands Church in particular has willingly embraced change. From the first day I walked into my new office, the people here have been eager to innovate, to grow, and to open themselves to a new day under God. I believe that is a tribute to progressive lay leadership, to an excellent staff, and to my ministerial predecessors. For all of them I am profoundly grateful. We all recognize that the church is not a laboratory for experimentation, but the very Body of Christ, growing in grace and attempting to live out the faith with which we are entrusted.

Finally, I am deeply appreciative of the many fellow pastors who have befriended and mentored me along the way.

ACKNOWLEDGMENTS

Over the years I have found an incredible generosity from
ministers in multiple denominations who have shared with
me their practice of ministry and, more important, the reasoning behind all of the programs and emphases and practices. This I have attempted to pass on through this work. I
have gleaned everywhere, but no vineyard has proved
more fertile than the work of Lyle Schaller, who has been
my mentor from afar for many years through his writings
and has become a friend in more recent days.

FOREWORD

What is the best way to learn how to minister with new generations of people in a new millennium? What is the most helpful way for congregational leaders to discover how to proclaim the gospel of Jesus Christ faithfully, effectively, and obediently in an age shaped increasingly by the fourth great religious awakening in American church history?

For at least four or five decades, the most common responses to these and similar questions referred to the continuing education programs for pastors offered by theological schools, denominational agencies, state universities, retreat centers, church-related colleges, and a variety of parachurch organizations.

The closing years of the twentieth century have moved two new options to the top of that list of resources. One is the self-identified teaching church, which has been inventing new approaches to ministry with new generations. Typically these teaching churches invite congregational leaders to come for a two- or three-day workshop. The leaders of the host church explain their philosophy of ministry, what they have been doing, why they do it that way, what the results have been, what they learned, and how they would do it differently if they were to do it over again. The visitors are encouraged to ask their own "how," "why," and "what" questions. The visiting learners also are encouraged to understand the difference between *adopt* and *adapt* as they return home and redesign their ministry plan. The visitors are challenged to think, to ask questions, and to discover new approaches to ministry.

A more accessible resource is the autobiographical

account of the life and ministry of one congregation. That explains the birth of this series, Innovators in Ministry. In the first volume in this series, Randy Frazee describes in *The Comeback Congregation* how a congregation that had lost nearly a thousand members was renewed through a new vision for a new day. In *Spiritual Entrepreneurs,* Michael Slaughter explains the six principles that enabled a rural, open country congregation to grow from an average worship attendance of fewer than a hundred to over three thousand in less than two decades. How do you do church in a downtown environment? Howard Edington answers that question with a thrilling account of what has been happening at First Presbyterian Church in Orlando, Florida. His autobiographical account, *Downtown Church,* is filled with signs of hope for that type of congregation.

In this volume, Richard Dunagin answers many of the most difficult questions being asked today.

How does the new pastor become the spiritual leader of a congregation? For well over three centuries one answer was, "That goes with the office. When you move into the parsonage or manse, that role and responsibility goes with the franchise." A second response was, "Outlive your predecessor and all the old pillars who retain a loyalty to your predecessor."

In today's world the answer is, "You earn it!" In the first chapter, Dr. Dunagin explains how the combination of creativity, hard work, and commitment to the power of Scripture can enable that newly arrived pastor to earn the role of spiritual leader.

How does one build a large congregation in a culture that places a premium on diversity? One way is to conceptualize it as a congregation of congregations of groups, classes, choirs, circles, cells, fellowships, and organizations. The beginning point for accomplishing that, as the author explains, is to offer meaningful choices in worship—and that is the theme of the fourth chapter.

A persuasive argument can be made that the most distinctive single characteristic of the contemporary religious revival in America is not the growing number of prayer cells or adult Bible study groups or megachurches or religious programs on network television or laypersons choosing a Christian vocation as a second career. The unique component of this fourth great awakening is the growing number of congregations that have been able to redefine the definition of church from a building to a network of worshiping communities. More and more congregations gather people together for the corporate worship of God in two or three or five or ten or fifty or two hundred different locations every weekend. How can that be accomplished? Read chapter 5 to discover that, while it is not easy, it can be done.

One of the most widely used words today to describe what people are seeking in a culture filled with anonymity is "connected." People want to feel connected to God, to God's church, to others, to a worshiping community, to something that helps them find meaning in life, and to their feelings. How can this be accomplished? Can it be done through preaching? How will people respond? In the sixth chapter of this book, the author offers an innovative strategy to respond to that desire to feel connected.

Why would anyone want to read this book about an obscure congregation in Texas? One reason is that we can learn from peers. This is a book by a pastor who has studied, learned, prayed, worked, suffered, and rejoiced in doing parish ministry. It is filled with lessons from experiences.

It also is important to note that the Lake Highlands congregation is not a megachurch. It is a congregation with which most readers can identify.

Second, the central theme speaks to a basic problem confronting most congregations today. That problem is an absence of focus. Without that clearly and precisely defined focus on what God is calling this congregation to be and to be doing, the natural tendency is to drift into tomorrow.

Third, the best chapter in the book speaks in autobiographical terms to a critical factor in leadership. In the tenth chapter the author explains how an error in tactics can undermine a commendable goal *and how that error can be corrected.* From this pilgrim's perspective this is the most valuable lesson in this book.

Fourth, the twentieth century saw the churches focus increasingly on individuals: teenagers, women, missions, clergy, educators, single adults, men, children, choir members, elders, deacons, seekers, disciples, learners, widows, inquirers, and others. The day has arrived when more congregations must change their focus from individuals to family constellations. The last chapter describes how one congregation is beginning to design a strategy to do this.

Finally, as the author points out early in the book, this congregation has been swimming uphill against the demographic tide. The easy approach to the twenty-first century would have been for this congregation to grow smaller in numbers and older in the age of the membership. That numerical decline could have been explained by changes in housing patterns and in the composition of the surrounding population.

How can a congregation swim upstream against the tide? An effective response to that question requires a high level of intentionality in defining purpose and in designing a ministry plan, a far above average degree of creativity, an openness to new ideas, a venturesome spirit, an exceptionally large amount of patience and persistence, a willingness to challenge people with what many perceive to be unattainable goals, and a driving conviction that God is at work in his world.

That is why we invite you to read this volume in the Innovators in Ministry series.

Lyle E. Schaller
Naperville, Illinois

INTRODUCTION

Unlike most ministers, I did not grow up in the church. Most of my early church experiences came as the result of various friends' invitations to visit their congregations. I had a natural hunger for God and was actually baptized on four different occasions in four different churches. Nevertheless, my ties with the people of God were dependent upon who was in my class at school in any particular year.

As a senior in high school, I had a profound religious conversion that began a process of radical transformation. Answering the call to ministry, I knew instinctively that part of my life's mission would be to reach people like myself, those who did not have the advantage of a strong church background.

In every congregation where I have been assigned, I have sought new ways to reach into the community with the good news of God. In 1990 my bishop appointed me to a nonpastoral role as the director of church extension for our annual conference. In that capacity I encountered numerous other creative and outreaching persons in several denominations. I also met Lyle Schaller, who has immeasurably expanded my horizons. Many of these persons have served as models or mentors, greatly increasing my competency.

In the summer of 1994 I was invited by my bishop to apply whatever learnings and experiences I had to a local setting in Dallas, Texas. Lake Highlands Church had a membership of 1,700 and an average attendance of less than 450. The normal trajectory of a congregation situated in a fully built-out neighborhood of a major metropolitan area, such as that of Lake Highlands, ranges from stagnation to decline. We have been able to reverse the trend, increasing our attendance by 60 percent in four years and steadily growing in membership.

This chronicle of our turnaround has a broader purpose than mere self-congratulation; we want to encourage the legions of local congregations located in nongrowing settings to a new beginning. Plainly stated, stagnation and decline are not inevitable. Most churches are simply not situated in rapidly growing suburban communities where hordes of newly arrived families are eager to join up. Quite the contrary, the vast majority of American churches worship and work in rather stable communities that experience population shifts (for example, Asians replacing Anglos, or Hispanics replacing African Americans), but where the total population of "folks like us" does not markedly increase. It is to just such churches that I would offer our congregation as an example of hope.

Two main audiences, then, are envisioned. First, I want to address local church ministers. Every pastor I have ever met begins ministry with a burning in the soul to change the world for Christ. Yet after several years, many of these same faithful men and women have become discouraged. They are barely hanging on where they are currently serving and expend a great deal of energy fantasizing about some new place of ministry. "If only I could get a *real* church in a growing area, then things would be better." As with many of my compatriots, I have never enjoyed the opportunity to serve a church in a growing suburban community. Instead, every congregation I have pastored has been located in a stable, transitional, or declining neighborhood. I learned early on that if I were to find any real-life satisfaction in my ministry, it would not come from my next appointment but from a combination of creativity and hard work in my present difficult place. In this work I attempt to show some of both, including some of my failures and how I dealt with them. Baring one's soul is always risky, but many generous local church pastors have done this for me, and I feel obligated to share my experiences with fellow pastors.

The other audience for this book is the local church-planning committee. For true advancement to occur, even a highly competent and well-motivated pastor is not enough. Rather, the lay leadership of the church must be energized. Due to a lack of insight, often a stagnant congregation will simply assume that their basic problem is that the current minister is just not duplicating what the pastor did in the golden era in that congregation's history. "If only we could hire a new minister who would repeat Reverend Smith's style from back in 1954, we would be a great church again." The world today is immeasurably more complicated than it was in 1954, and yesterday's methods will not accomplish tomorrow's dreams. As they read through this volume, I hope that local church leaders will capture a sense of some of the issues facing us, and in seeing how one congregation has addressed them, unleash their own creativity under God. At Lake Highlands we have "colored outside the lines." That is because the lines have been drawn too narrowly and our stagnant ways have excluded many of the precious people we so much want to reach.

My modest prayer is that this book will catalyze congregational leaders—ministerial and lay—to swim upstream, or to change the metaphor, to move beyond the walls for Christ.

CHAPTER 1

THE EXPLOSIVE POWER OF *TNT*

Two questions confronted me as I was installed as the senior pastor at Lake Highlands United Methodist Church in the summer of 1994. First, *How can I as a new pastor become established as the spiritual leader of the people assigned to my care?* A congregation will come to identify its leader in some way or another, but my goal was to become the spiritual leader since that is the business we are in. The second and related issue was this, *How can I get my folks to actually study the Bible, the source for our spiritual development?* After all, it does no good for me to become the spiritual leader if no one is willing to follow along a spiritual track. Yes, all Christian ministers encourage the congregation under their charge to commit themselves to Christian discipleship through Bible study. Yet all too few Christians actually do study Scripture, at least in any systematic manner that helps us to grasp its truths and to apply them to daily living.

Trivia That Transforms

I chanced upon two incredibly powerful pieces of trivia one day, not powerful in themselves but dynamite when combined with each other. That combination has transformed my congregation. Those two items are these: first, there are 260 chapters in the New Testament; and second, there are 260 weekdays in the normal year (leap year being excluded). "What would happen," I asked myself, "if we got our church members to commit themselves to reading the New Testament, the most important document ever written, one chapter a day on weekdays only, leaving Saturday to 'catch up on last Tuesday's reading' and Sunday to go to church? What if our people were literally 'all on the same page together' in their Bibles? Might we stimulate spiritual discussions across generations and among peoples who otherwise have nothing else in common? Might we actually build a sense of community around the Book, rather than simply around some social activity or some personality?" The prospects were mind-boggling.

But how to keep people on track, that was the question. In order to meet the challenge, Dr. Timothy Walker, a long-time friend and colleague, joined in my venture. Together we set ourselves the task of creating what became known as *TNT (Through the New Testament)*.[1] This was more than a gimmick; we embarked on a complete strategy to make spiritual development a multifaceted reality. *TNT* has four basic components.

Phase One: Daily Bible Reading

At the most basic level of the *TNT* approach is individual Bible study. A daily assignment is made for each weekday. But the assignments are not simply, "Now I must read Matthew, followed by Mark, on the heels of which would be Luke, and now it is April 22 and I am tired of reading what seems like the same thing for the third time!" Let's face it, the synoptics can become monotonous to the novice Bible student. Thus, for our study, we began with Matthew but followed it with 1 Corinthians, and then 1 John, and so forth. We interspersed long books with short books for a sense of movement, and took only one Gospel per quarter. The *TNT* arrangement allows us to read the Passion narrative in the last five chapters of Luke during Holy Week, the five weekdays leading up to Easter.

To assist our Bible students in their understanding of the Scriptures they were reading daily, we published a pocket-sized notebook that contains a single page for each chapter of the New Testament. [2] Along with each day's assignment is a brief, pithy commentary, which helps the reader to unpack the most important or otherwise difficult aspects of the day's passage. But Bible facts are not enough; thus, each chapter contains some very pointed, personal application questions. The page is rounded off with a Thought for the Day, which reinforces a key theme of the text.

In the back of the notebook are twelve Check-Up Sheets, one for each month. The *TNT* participant is instructed to complete the check-up sheet and turn it in to the church office. At the end of the year, the church may elect to award certificates of completion. How exciting it is for a sixty-two-year-old church member to stand beside a twenty-two-year-old, each of whom has just finished reading the entire New Testament for the first time in their lives!

Phase Two: Small Group Sharing

Individual Bible study is crucial and forms the foundation for our own spiritual development, but its value can be enhanced. One way to "get more out of it" is to "give it away." We do not know as well or believe as deeply that which we only think about inwardly. Articulating an insight both crystallizes the thought and seals it in the heart. Accordingly, *TNT* encourages its adherents to form small discussion groups. The most natural way to utilize *TNT* in a group setting is simply to permit participants to share their answers to the life application questions dealt with throughout the week. No Bible study "leader" is necessary; in fact, someone who explains all the mysteries in the text is the antithesis of what is needed here. Rather, each person should be encouraged to take a turn at sharing insights gleaned in the study. These small groups (six to ten persons each) can meet in homes weekly, biweekly, or on any other desired schedule. Some limited training in facilitating a small group is helpful (e.g., "How do I deal with Tommy Talkative?"), but minimal Bible knowledge is necessary to launch a successful group. Many new insights and applications will come as the members pool their week's learnings together.

Phase Three: Pastor's Bible Study

As the author of the *TNT* materials, I quickly became identified within my new congregation as a Bible scholar. But I was not yet the spiritual leader I wanted to become. Thus, to further capitalize on the *TNT*-led spiritual development, I launched a Wednesday "Pastor's Bible Study. " Actually, I held two identical sessions each Wednesday, one in the morning and one in the evening. During this time, I presented an exegesis of the five chapters of Scripture that had just been completed, the assigned readings for the previous Wednesday through Tuesday. This is the first of the two ways in which my congregation began to see me as their spiritual leader, for I was able to unpack, in a much deeper way than was possible in the one-page *TNT* commentary, the passages under consideration. Weekly, throughout the whole of 1995, I spent one full hour answering questions that piqued their interest and spoon-feeding these disciples-in-the-making. Incidentally, it is in just such a teaching forum (as opposed to a preaching occasion) that I find exposition is most effective. Here were people asking, "What does this passage mean?" My job was to feed their hunger with the bread of life. I did not hand this assignment over to my associate pastor because I recognized that this was my opportunity to establish myself as the spiritual leader of my flock.

A side note: Since *TNT* has been developed, many other churches have used it with great benefit for their members. I have strongly encouraged the senior pastors of these congregations to offer their own *TNT* Pastor's Bible Study, not only to establish their credentials as the spiritual leader of their flock but for an additional reason. *TNT* is written from a particular theological position—not implying that it is doctrinaire, but simply acknowledging that, like all human beings, the authors have particular biases and ways of understanding Scripture. Because we all differ somewhat, doubtless there will be some interpretations that are totally disagreeable to the pastor who encourages its use in the church. The Pastor's Bible Study offers a forum in which the pastor in charge may "correct" any "bad" theology found in *TNT*.

A testimonial: Although my coauthor and I are on the same theological wavelength, there are nuances of disagreement between us. The lay readers in my church could never detect them, except that on occasion I have said to my Pastor's Bible Study, "I think a slightly different spin should be thrown upon this passage." I would be disappointed if Tim has not reciprocated. In fact, my own understanding of Scripture has changed, matured as I would rather think of it, and the time may come when I need to "correct" my own writing! Therefore, a Pastor's Bible Study is very helpful for offering the local pastor's own perspective on the Bible.

Phase Four: Preaching the *TNT* "Lectionary"

The second way in which I became identified as the spiritual leader of my congregation through the *TNT* strategy was to preach every Sunday throughout 1995 from a passage taken from one of the week's five assigned chapters. *TNT* served as a sort of lectionary for the year, not nearly as limited as the normal lectionaries with which we are familiar, and one that was actually being read by almost half of my active membership. I announced before the year began that this was my intention, so that the members were encouraged in every way to study for themselves, to teach each other through their small group experiences, and to learn in an intensive way through my weekly pastor-led Bible study as well as in the worship service.

I deviated from the text only once, and that during the Advent season, although I would have felt free to deviate on other occasions if circumstances dictated. But the preaching component was the crowning piece of a completed puzzle. The pulpit is the premier place that a pastor establishes the spiritual leadership that is desired. But its effect is multiplied immeasurably when that pastor takes a text that the people have wrestled with privately and in small groups and speaks forth the truth of God's Word in a way that zeros in on the human drama of these disciples' lives. It is much more likely in such a setting that the greatest possible miracle of communication may occur: that through the words of a human being, the Word of God may speak!

Not everyone in our church read *TNT* individually. Of those who did, not all joined a small group; neither did everyone attend the midweekly Bible study. But enough did that when the preaching came from a lived-with text, everyone's ears perked up. Indeed, *TNT* has caused an explosion of discipleship within Lake Highlands United Methodist Church, thank God!

CHAPTER 2

WHAT ARE WE HERE FOR?

How do you know when something is scheduled? is a normal question for any newcomer to ask, especially if the newcomer is to assume the title of senior pastor. But the answer I received that first week at Lake Highlands United Methodist Church was quite startling. Boiled down, it came out something like this: "You have to go ask each board, council, commission, committee, ministry, class, or group—individually."

In 1994 there was no master calendar. Furthermore, no centralized body was in charge of determining whether or not there was any conflict in the various ventures that were scheduled, other than the advice of the Business Administrator who logged room requests into the computer. The depth of the problem became all too apparent when, on the same Sunday morning that summer, one group hosted a breakfast for the entire congregation as a fund-raiser in the Family Life Building, while a second group offered a free breakfast to anyone who would come—their means of bringing new people into their group. Clearly, order was needed in our chaotic setting.

No Centralized Mission

Less obvious, but even more crucial, was the lack of a centralized mission. Some of our groups were (at least by the perception of others) only interested in advancing their own private agendas. Two examples: first, we have an unusually strong Boy Scout Troop, 129 boys and 121 adult leaders at last count. Rather than feeling a sense of (holy) pride in the group, many Lake Highlands Church members have been critical, finding fault with the amount of space the troop requires every Monday night, the scuffs they leave on the floors, and the holes they leave in Sunday school class attendance on their camp-out weekends each month, especially in the confirmation class. Many church members have expressed deep resentment for the troop.

Second, we have a twenty-plus–year tradition of producing the ACT (Actors of Christian Talent) youth musical each February or March. Our community offers excellent music programs in the local public schools; consequently, the production of a Broadway musical has been a big and successful part of our youth program each year. However, once again, there are detractors. The normal youth programming gets short shrift during the two to three months of rehearsals and performances. Set construction has often monopolized the Fellowship Hall for a month to six weeks, displacing other groups. Some church members note (correctly) that many youth participate only in the ACT musical and do not otherwise darken the doors of the church. "So why should we knock ourselves out and put up with all this for nothing?" has been asked on more than one occasion, by church members and staff alike.

The problem in 1994 was a lack of focus. Although it was unseen, that same problem plagued a number of the committees and groups even closer to the traditional center of the church's ministry. Rather than operating as a united whole, we actually functioned as a collection of small duchies, each operating semi-autonomously, each with its own agenda. No one was asking the most basic of questions: "Why do we exist? What is the 'Church,' written with a capital C, and who are we in this local congregation?" Everyone doubtless had answers, but not all the answers were the same, and no single answer was guiding our common life.

One observation I have made in this regard has been confirmed to me repeatedly over many years of ministry: "When people have no cause bigger than themselves, they will fight." That was the underlying issue at Lake Highlands. No central cause bigger than ourselves was guiding us. It was every person (or group) for themselves. Such a chaotic schema inevitably leads to low morale, as well as to competition over valued resources. Lake Highlands, like many other congregations, had stepped off of its theological underpinnings of a biblical purpose for its existence and was tottering on the edge of a self-destructive precipice of multiple, competing purposes. Clearly, we needed a central mission to guide us.

A Mission Statement Is Not Enough

Let me hasten to say, however, that what we lacked was not a "Mission Statement." In fact, we had one of those already, drafted only a year before my arrival. Yes, we had a mission statement; what we lacked was a mission. Our mission statement (which ultimately we will have to revise) is quite lengthy. It spells out in rather elevated language a lot of important things that the church is about. But its value was negligible when it came to guiding the community. One can see the deficiencies of our mission statement when one reads that, among other things, it is the mission of Lake Highlands United Methodist Church "to support the district, annual conference and other connectional activities of The United Methodist Church." Do we really exist in order to keep the regional and national judicatories well-oiled? Our statement also says that we exist "to create, maintain and ensure the proper preservation of membership rolls and other appropriate records." Yes, these things have some importance, but if this is our mission, we exist only to be a bureaucracy!

Moving Toward a Mission

How to address the issue of a central mission? That was my dilemma.

Every new pastor goes into that new setting with a certain amount of *moral capital*. The people are generally ready for a new leader whenever he or she moves in. After all, most of the time when there is a change of pastors, it is because someone (either the former pastor or the congregational leaders) was unhappy. Congregations usually start out hopeful that their new leader will be excellent, and they are frequently willing to give that leader the benefit of the doubt. We often refer to those first several months as the *honeymoon period*. Some "experts" counsel new leaders to refrain from changing anything during the first year, advice that I believe is terribly misguided. Unless one's predecessor was considered a saint who literally died in the pulpit while converting an avowed satanist with his last breath, the new pastor is likely to be given a "limited-time blank check" to assert leadership. A pastor who waits a year before instituting change is squandering the best opportunity that is likely to be available for years to come. The first year is the best time to bring strategic change. Of course, one must not walk too far out in front of the people; such persons are called martyrs, not prophets or leaders!

With such an understanding, I "struck" early on. I utilized the incident of the competing breakfasts to talk about our need for a centralized scheduling system. But more important, I used the occasion as a launching point to talk about the mission of the church. The time and occasion: a fall planning retreat in my third month. The participants: all of the key leaders from each of the various work areas of our church. As the newly installed pastor, these key lay workers looked to me for leadership. My message that day can be condensed into the following:

If I come to any of your places of employment on Monday morning, I am certain that you would be able to tell me what business your company is in and what your individual function is within the organization. Further, every employee and every division of your corporation contributes to the main mission of the company. Any parts of the company that do not contribute to the main mission, and especially those that actually detract from the mission, are out of line and would not be tolerated by your management.

For example, if you work for General Motors, you know that you are in the transportation business, and that your own job of installing passenger-side doors contributes to the main mission of building transportation vehicles. If two other workers further down the assembly line were removing half of the doors that you had just mounted, pretty soon a supervisor would approach them to correct their actions because they are detracting from the main mission of building transportation vehicles.

Now let me ask you, "What business is our church in? And what is the main mission of the church? That is, what is so vital that if it is not done, we will fail to be the church?"

After that is settled, then we must address these two additional questions: "In what way is the group that you represent contributing to the main mission? And in what ways can we 'tweak' your group to make it better aligned to our mission?"

Much of the input I gave to the body that day came from a "Quest for Quality" workshop which was conducted for leaders in my annual conference by Ezra Earl Jones, General Secretary of the General Board of Discipleship of

The United Methodist Church. He had helped to clarify my own thinking about the church. Boiled down to its essence, the main "business" of the church is people, and our mission, the reason we exist, is "to assist each other in becoming disciples of Jesus Christ." In order to fulfill this primary task of disciple-making, we must, in all of our efforts, embody a fourfold process: (1) reach out and receive those who have no relationship with God in Christ; (2) relate them to God; (3) nurture them in the faith; and (4) send them out in service to the world in Christ's name. Anything that advances the cause of disciple-making is on target; anything that fails to advance this mission is out of line and must be changed.

A Stirring Response

The schema was simple, but the response was electrifying. Suddenly our congregation's leaders began to see themselves engaged in a glorious and noble common effort. Rather than being individual groups in competition with one another, we reconceptualized ourselves as partners in a grand enterprise. Our real need was not to defeat other groups in a Christianized zero-sum game, where if one succeeds, another must fail. Rather, we saw the need to reorient our many ministries, programs, and groups around this central axis. Thus, no longer were the Scouts to be seen as being in competition with the confirmation Sunday school class for attendance once every month. Instead, we found ourselves invited to "tweak" the system. Perhaps we might give the Scouts' chaplain a copy of our confirmation materials and ask him to coordinate his camp devotions around the same theme being used back home that week. We began asking ourselves, "Can we find ways to make allies of our fellow groups?" And rather than complain about the ACT musical, why not envision ways to incorporate disciple-making as the prime reason for the musical? Perhaps we could encourage the use of more "spiritual" plays, add the youth director to the body of ACT workers in order to reach kids who came only to this production, and the like. All of a sudden we were talking about helping each other to be successful. The key was to redefine "success" around the main mission of the church.

No, the Kingdom did not come. But we have begun to develop a very different spirit about ourselves. Since that fateful fall retreat, I have sought to model this new understanding. I have become the first Lake Highlands pastor to go on a Scout camp-out, which I now do at least once annually. Likewise, I have participated as an adult volunteer (in a very small way) for the ACT musical production. I affirm these two ministries publicly and encourage others to participate. This is my attempt to teach graphically, "No group around here is an enemy; our goal is to assist each other to be successful at disciple-making." We hear much less criticism from the church members about these two groups, and the groups themselves are more cooperative with the rest of the church. For example, the most recent ACT production did not displace the contemporary worship service, which now also meets in the fellowship hall, even on the day of the Sunday afternoon matinee. And we continue to look for ways to "tweak" our ministries to make them more productive in fulfilling the main mission to make disciples for Jesus Christ.

Transforming the Naturally Conservative Trustees and Finance Committee

Some parts of the church system do not contribute directly to disciple-making. The nature of the work done by a local church's Board of Trustees and its Finance Committee does not readily lend itself to such a task. These two bodies are, in fact, almost always the two most conservative bodies in any institution, and often they become blockers to the advancement of the institution's mission. The Finance Committee may respond without any creative thinking, "No, we can't take on any new programs or hire any new staff; we don't have the funds." Similarly, the Trustees may say, "Those neighborhood kids are tearing up the place; we cannot hold such a program in our church building." What can be done?

The best way I have discovered to remove this blockage is to transform the self-identity of these two bodies. They need to reconceptualize themselves as "energy loops" whose function is to propel the main mission forward. Our Board of Trustees and Committee on Finance now understand that their job is not to guard the church's resources or to save up for a rainy day, but to help enable the mission of disciple-making. They do this by raising adequate funds for the work and by dedicating the facilities to those programs and ministries that most advance the cause. Our Finance Committee now sees itself as carrying out a charge to raise whatever money is needed, not to inhibit the flow of funds. Likewise, our Trustees see themselves as dedicated to providing attractive, functional facilities that will best enable the main mission of disciple-making to be fulfilled.

The mission of the church must become paramount in the thinking of the entire organization. The Trustees themselves can be ignited by inviting them to think about new ministries that we might develop to further our outreach. "Do we need to build new buildings or redesign our existing facilities? How are newcomers likely to respond when they first enter our facility? Is our signage okay; do we make a good first impression?" Likewise, the Finance Committee should be asking the Evangelism Committee if they have adequate funding. "Can we raise additional monies for you?" Although this may seem a bit unreal to those who have suffered through years of institutional blockage, let me assure you that even the most conservative committee can be transformed when a mission bigger than ourselves energizes our activities because it has captured our imagination.

Of course, it is always wise to reward those who share in the mission. That is, I often share stories in the midst of the dryness of a monthly Board of Trustees or Finance Committee meeting—stories about lives that have been transformed because "we made room for that new ministry in our facilities" or stories about "the new staff member that we strained to hire; she has just launched a new Bible study for children in an apartment complex." No greater reward can come than to know that we have each contributed something valuable to the mission, that through the facilities we've devoted and through the money we've dedicated (the provinces of Trustees and Finance, respectively), precious souls have advanced on their journeys as growing disciples. After all, we are all in this together, making disciples for Jesus Christ.

CHAPTER 3

WHO ARE THE PEOPLE IN YOUR NEIGHBORHOOD?

Our church is a fairly comfortable place to be—that is, if you are a middle- to upper-middle-class white homeowner, preferably from a two-parent family. Newcomers to our church are more likely to feel at home if they meet these criteria, especially if they come with a fairly extensive church background. Of course, almost any Lake Highlands member will tell you that we are always happy to include folks who are different from ourselves, and indeed, we boast of a small number of Asian, Hispanic, and African American families, as well as a handful of African members. Likewise, we have several single-parent households, as well as numerous single persons, especially those who are over 65 years of age. We even see a few relatively poor persons in our sanctuary at eleven o'clock on Sunday morning. Nevertheless, the percentage of persons who differ significantly from our typical demographic mix is small. Why?

As a first response, many of our members will say that it is because we reflect our neighborhood, that we are a large "neighborhood church," and that "most of the folks in our neighborhood must be similar to us." Indeed, almost all Lake Highlands attendees on a typical Sunday actually come from within a four-mile radius. But how representative are we of the larger community in which we are situated? Is our neighborhood 98 percent white? Is the vast majority of the adult population married? Do all of our community's families earn a middle- to upper-middle-class income? Do most of our neighbors own their own homes? Again, many of our folks, especially if standing in the church foyer, would answer with at least a qualified yes. However, if these same respondents were asked the same questions while they were shopping at any of our local supermarkets, and especially if they were standing in the halls of our local public schools, a radically different response might be given. I say that the response "might" be different, but not for everyone. Some of us seem to wear blinders when it comes to seeing people who are different from ourselves. For example, in my former job on the bishop's staff, I once worked with a declining church in a relatively small community, a church that had no members under age 65. The pastor lamented that there were no young families and no children in his community; therefore, his church could not grow. After conducting a brief demographic study, we informed this minister of the good news that the local elementary school had a rather sizable enrollment. The pastor quickly dismissed these statistics by saying that those children were obviously all bussed in. "None of them live around here." Next we assembled the most recent census data (then two years old) for the census tract in which the church's building is located, as well as the adjoining census tracts. Each of these revealed a large number of young families and a growing number of children living right there in the neighborhood. When the pastor was informed of this piece of good news, he fired back, "The government always gets stuff wrong, don't they!" No amount of persuasion could convince this blinded leader that the community outside the church's four walls was really different from that inside. They were old, so the community must likewise be old.

Lake Highlands Demographics

The three primary zip codes surrounding our church contain in excess of 110,000 people disbursed in some 63,000 households, according to the latest census. Of these, the majority are white, accounting for 69 percent of the whole. But a strong African American contingency can be found here (19 percent), joined by a rapidly growing 8 percent Hispanic and 4 percent Asian. When the next census is conducted, I suspect that even more dramatic changes will be noted. Perhaps the most startling transition yet documented in our community occurred during the 1980s, when the federal government sponsored rent subsidies for newly constructed apartments, which seemed to spring up on every piece of vacant ground in Lake Highlands. Within a decade we went from being a neighborhood of homeowners, in which more than 52 percent of all households lived in single-family housing, to a neighborhood of multifamily housing. The decline was so rapid that by 1990 barely 26 percent of neighborhood residents lived in single-family dwellings. Our neighborhood today is virtually built-out, with very little available land left. Thus, since 1990, few new homes (or apartments, for that matter) have been constructed. We are stalemated with what is perceived to be an overabundance of apartments. This is not greatly different from most urban areas, but it does represent a change to this particular neighborhood from previous years, a change that has been acutely felt and widely lamented.

A backlash occurred during the 1990s, when homeowners sought assistance from elected officials, asking them to "do something about our apartment problem." The perception that apartment residents do not create good neighborhoods is widely held within the Lake Highlands community, and there is at least some evidence to support this contention. Persons who rent tend to be far more transient than homeowners. In the state of Texas, for example, more than half of all renters have moved within the previous sixteen months, compared to just 10 percent of homeowners. This makes sense; it is difficult to sell a house and move in a short period of time, whereas it is relatively simple to change apartments. Stability, then, is an issue. Those who frequently move tend not to join organizations of any kind—PTA, service clubs, or churches. Likewise, crime, truancy, and a host of other social ills are overrepresented within the apartment community; no doubt this trend is tied to the relative poverty of its residents and the large number of single-parent homes concentrated there. This has caused great consternation for longer-term residents, many of whom are members of churches like ours.

To summarize, a once tightly knit community began to feel itself coming unraveled throughout the 1980s and 1990s. Although the overall population, which was growing up to and through the 1980s, has now stabilized, mobility rates are much higher today than in previous decades. People do not stay put for a lifetime. Lake Highlands Church, which had a fairly easy time attracting new residents who were purchasing new homes throughout the single-family building boom, found its growth leveling off by the mid-1980s, when apartments were under construction rather than new homes. Many younger families were moving to neighborhoods further removed from the troubles of the city.

If our church mirrors only half (or, more likely, one-fourth) of our neighborhood, who is reaching the other precious souls living in our midst? Is any church making disciples of the poor? Where are ethnic persons hearing the Word of God proclaimed? Who is loving the apartment dwellers? Into what part of the Christian family do single persons fit? And how can any congregation reach those folks who have no church background?

These were questions that I knew needed answers even before I arrived on the scene at Lake Highlands. In my previous position as the church extension officer for my annual conference, I had the privilege to learn a great deal about demographics and about the kinds of persons that mainline denominations are reaching. I also had the opportunity to network with some extremely gifted and experienced persons who were wrestling with similar questions. Some of these experts were from my own tradition, whereas others came from various denominational backgrounds. What I soon discovered was that my counterparts at the Baptist General Convention of Texas were light-years ahead of any Methodists I knew in both their sophistication at data gathering and their assimilation of the data to make sense of the real world. Among the brightest was Dr. Charles Lee Williamson, Director of the Missions Division of the Baptist General Convention of Texas. Under his leadership, his denomination was creating more than one hundred new congregations per year in my state. In contrast, my denomination counted it a good year when we planted five. The Baptists were extremely focused on reaching new people with the gospel of Christ, including ethnic persons, apartment dwellers, the poor, and others whom most churches could never reach. Their strategies were targeted to the individual group they were trying to reach because they knew that "one size" does not "fit all." They had learned to tailor their new congregations to the lifestyle of the people they sought to reach.

Williamson's Social Class Theory of Churching[1]

For purposes of analysis, American society can be subdivided into nine socioeconomic levels. At the top level are persons with incomes of $175,000 or more per year and/or a Ph.D. degree. The varying gradations go from this level to the bottom rung, which is characterized by a poverty-level (or less) income and/or an eighth-grade (or less) education. Persons in each of the nine levels have different life experiences, from ski trips to Europe for those at Level 1 to survival in unheated homes at Level 9. The greater the difference in level, the more radical the difference in people's lives.

In voluntary social settings people tend to congregate amongst others who are most like themselves. The old adage, "Birds of a feather flock together," holds more than a grain of truth. In general, people will socialize across no more than one-third of the nine-point scale. This is true in the clubs they join, the friendship networks they develop, and in the churches they attend. Sometimes there are exceptions; yet these often make the principle more obvious, as when a 700-member upper-middle-class congregation has a very poor member—one. The general population is certainly not composed of 700 to 1, upper-middle-class to poor. Exceptions are more likely to be found in working-class churches with a sprinkling of relatively young, upper-middle-class members. These are usually persons who themselves have working-class roots but who have experienced upward mobility. Chances are, as their own children grow up, this newer generation will not be content to continue attending the working-class church where their parents feel so at home.

Just as individual churches tend to be composed of a rather narrow range of socioeconomic classes, whole denominations likewise draw most of their membership from persons who are similar in their socioeconomic status. Obviously there is more variety across a denomination than in an individual congregation; nevertheless, the bulk of any given denomination's constituency is generally composed of persons of similar socioeconomic status.[2] As given groups have attained upward mobility, so too have the churches they attend.

For example, the Southern Baptist denomination at the close of World War II was chiefly composed of persons who were below the midpoint range on the nine-point scale. A major issue at the Texas State Convention during the mid-1950s was whether to seat a delegation from a large church in which the choir wore robes! ("Have they become 'high church' and lost the 'true faith'?") This conflict reflected the tension caused by the rapid upward mobility of much of that denomination's constituency. Southern Baptists as a whole, like other denominations before them, were upwardly mobile. Today that denomination is well above the midpoint of the scale; most Baptist church choirs now wear robes. Accordingly, the issues currently addressed by the Southern Baptist Convention are very different, yet they are still related to the culture of the membership—only now their concerns reflect a middle- and upper-middle-class agenda.

Congregations made up of persons from lower on the socioeconomic scale do not function in the same manner as those from higher socioeconomic groups. One of the basic differences is in the size of the congregations they tend to form. In general, the higher the social class (up to but not including the highest class), the larger the congregation that is likely to be formed. Conversely, the lower the social class, the smaller the congregation. Of course, there are numerous exceptions (e.g., many small churches com- prised of a middle-class membership), but it is indeed rare to find a large church made up of poorer members.

There appear to be at least four reasons for this phenom- enon. First, poorer persons are more likely to form larger congregations only if they have a combination of hope and the dream of upward mobility, either for themselves and/or for their children. Without hope, there is no sense of security, which is a necessary ingredient in forming an alliance with a large company of strange faces in a big church setting. (I will say more about this need for a sense of security later.) The plain fact, however, is that hope is often in short supply in poorer communities, where one's efforts often go unrewarded and where dreams are often dashed. Thus, without hope, few large congregations are found among the poor.

Second, poorer persons are seldom found in "traditional churches" of any size; but when hope-filled, though poor, people ingrain themselves in what Dr. Robert Fogel terms "enthusiastic religions," they may join larger congregations. Some "Spirit-filled" congregations are thus able to bridge a broad range of socioeconomic, racial, and ethnic barriers. Most congregations, however, are not able to offer this combination to those who live in poor neighborhoods. Likewise, their very enthusiasm is sometimes a turnoff to those who feel hopeless.

The third variable in the list of why poorer people seldom congregate in larger churches has to do with the fact that the poor tend not to be "joiners." Sociologists have long observed that people who join any organization tend to join more organizations, whereas other persons tend not to join anything. The inclination either to join or to avoid organizations is related to social class. That is, not only are organized religious groups bypassed by many poorer persons, but likewise the PTA, political action groups, civic clubs, and all other organizations find a smaller membership from society's lowest socioeconomic stratum.

The fourth reason why persons in the lower classes tend not to form larger congregations lies, I believe, at the heart of the matter. Simply stated, poorer persons tend not to trust. Without a basic sense of trust, people will not congregate in large numbers—for any reason. This begins to make sense when one considers the different life experiences of persons in lower socioeconomic circumstances compared with those of middle-class persons. For example, persons in poor communities know that they are charged more for groceries at their corner market than are their middle-class counterparts in the suburbs. They know their neighborhood schools are inferior. They know that at every moment they are being ripped off by society, and that at any moment they may be robbed or assaulted. Their life chances are not the same as those of middle-class persons. In short, they know that the world is not a safe place for them. Thus, it is not safe to congregate among strangers, whether in a neighborhood bar or even in a local church. An intersection in the poorest section of any major city may have four small bars, one on each corner, four small stores, or four small churches. Seldom will you find any large establishment of any description there. Lacking any sense of basic security, it is difficult to have hope (at least in this world). The cold, hard reality is that the deck seems stacked, and dreams have a way of turning into nightmares. Why join with enthusiasts when they seem detached from the paramount reality? Why join anything?

Conversely, middle-class persons, despite their fears of unknown terrors at work in the larger society, live in an environment of trust. Theirs is a world in which each person does his or her work (often in a large, complex office setting), trusting that the person in the next cubicle and those on the floors above and below are all likewise doing their jobs. Together, everyone profits. Thus, the higher one's rung on the socioeconomic ladder, the more involved the individual tends to be with larger social groups—on the job, in the PTA, in a political action group or service club, or in larger churches—in which a wide variety of needs are met. Thus, most large congregations are made up of middle- and upper-middle-class persons.

Interestingly, the situation often reverts back to the pattern of the lower class when one reaches the highest socioeconomic level. The very affluent seldom congregate in really large institutions. They, like the poor, tend not to trust. People are "after their money," seeking to rip them off as well. Thus, the wealthy tend not to take active roles in really large congregations, although more exceptions are found here than among the poor.

Denominations have their greatest growth when their constituents are rising into the middle class. The Congregationalist Church experienced such mobility during the 1790s; the Methodists followed in the 1890s; while the Southern Baptists did the same in the 1950s. In each era, the denomination whose constituency was then moving into the middle class grew the most. Thus, Methodists built two new churches per day in the 1880 and 1890 period. However, having attained middle-class status, Methodism ceased to appeal to the lower classes early in this century.

Evidence of Methodism's loss of interest in, and appeal to, the poor is found in the circumstances of the church split that led to the formation of the Church of the Nazarene. The issues were twofold: (a) theological— Methodism was becoming "too liberal," and (b) sociological—the early letterhead of the Nazarenes is illustrative here. It read, "The Church of the Nazarene: Proclaiming Christ in the Inner City." This new break-off denomination claimed that Methodism was abandoning the inner city— as early as 1910! Although The Methodist Church grew to be the largest Protestant denomination through the 1950s, today United Methodism is in decline, having lost in excess of two million members over the last two decades. This is in part due to the fact that this denomination has not appealed to the lower socioeconomic segment of our society, which makes up the bulk of the American population, in several decades.

Every major denomination today is middle-class (United Methodist, Baptist, Lutheran, and so forth) or higher (Congregationalist, Episcopalian, some Presbyterians). Most Americans today, however, are not in these socioeconomic categories. And for the first time in our history, younger generations no longer expect to exceed their parents' socioeconomic level. Thus, we find a curious phenomenon in U.S. Christendom: *All major denominations are attempting to reach the same, limited, and shrinking segment of the American population.* No major denomination, until very recently, has made a serious attempt to "church down" the socioeconomic ladder. All denominations have ministered to the lower classes, providing social welfare and justice ministries. But none have been successful at congregating significant numbers of persons from socioeconomic classes lower than their own.

Why reach the lower classes? There are at least three reasons for any denomination to attempt to establish congregations among the lower socioeconomic classes.

(1) *The bulk of the American population is found in the lower socioeconomic classes.* To fail to reach the poorer segments of our society is to overlook most of our citizens.

(2) *The gospel is authenticated when we care for those who cannot do anything for us in return.* Too often the church is accused of being interested only in money and in those who have money. But the gospel calls us to show our interest even in those who can do nothing for the church financially.

(3) *Reaching the poor is evidence that Christ is among us.* In answer to John's query about whether he was the Messiah, Jesus replied, "Go and tell John what you have seen and heard: the blind receive their sight, the lame walk...*the poor have good news brought to them*" (Luke 7:22, italics mine).

Reaching New People for Christ

It is apparent that, if we are to take seriously our mandate to "preach the gospel to everything in our territory that breathes," we must plan new strategies. Simply opening the doors to our buildings and hoping that the many differing peoples of the world will come is an inadequate approach. In fact, Jesus told us to *go to* the world, not to sit back and watch them come to us. Our tendency is to say, "Shame on them for not coming." I believe we ought instead to say, "Shame on us for not going."

At Lake Highlands we have been intentional in reaching new people in a variety of ways. In the next chapter you will read about alternative worship services, our attempt to reach persons who are socioeconomically similar to our congregation but who have little or no church background. And in the following chapter you will read about a far more radical plan to take the gospel to the people through Off-Campus Ministries. There, our target audiences are persons who are racially, ethnically, and socioeconomically different from our typical members. To be faithful, we must devise effective strategies to address all of the people in our neighborhood.

Jesus was once asked, "Who is my neighbor?" The answer he gave was actually a parable we now refer to as "the Good Samaritan." Here was a man who saw someone different from himself but nevertheless put himself out in order to help. On the PBS kids' program *Sesame Street*, Big Bird sometimes sings an important song: "Who are the people in your neighborhood... the people that you meet when you're walking down the street, the people that you meet each day?" It is essential that we learn who is in fact our neighbor. Churches can study demographic data from the Census Bureau, from their local school district, and from local government agencies. Most denominational headquarters can provide additional lifestyle data, and several private companies now sell data as well. We must do at least as well as Big Bird in knowing who those neighbors are if we are to fulfill Jesus' mandate to love our neighbors as ourselves.

But knowing about them is not the same as reaching them with the gospel. Too often we mistake the knowing for the doing. Jesus calls us not merely to learn who is in our neighborhoods, but to truly love by sharing the good news with all our neighbors. We are grasping for strategies to put love into practice.

CHAPTER 4

9:44 AND MORE

It's 9:44 on Sunday morning. The renovated Fellowship Hall, the church's original sanctuary, "begins to rock," as some of the younger faces in the crowd put it. An electric bass pounds out a rhythmic line with a driving beat. It is quickly joined by an electronic keyboard, an electric guitar, a full drum set, and on this morning, a soprano saxophone. The rhythms and harmonies are akin to those found on any rock station on the FM dial, but the lyrics that now begin are of a decidedly different flavor. Yes, they're love songs, all right, but the One celebrated is the great Lover of our souls, Jesus the Lord.

Contemporary worship began at Lake Highlands United Methodist Church in October 1995. The service is different in everything from its starting time, 9:44 A.M., to the way the offering is taken. When asked about the 9:44 start, my standard reply is: "A different time for a different service." Before the offering is received, visitors are encouraged not to give. "This is something we do in our church community to pay for the utilities and maintain our church," we explain. "You're our guests, and all we expect of you is that you pass the plate with a smile." This service also has a different target audience that it seeks to reach: primarily those who are baby boomers and younger (although some seventy-year-olds are faithful attenders), and especially those who have little or no experience in church. I believe that we must offer different kinds of services in order to reach different kinds of people.

People Don't Just *Act* Different, They Really *Are* Different

We have recognized that the world—even our little slice of the world—is not homogeneous. We have many people in our congregation who dearly love classical music, some of whom have taken me to enjoy the Dallas Symphony on occasion. But I suspect that, outside of the church, it is rather a small number of people, even on our part of the planet, who arise the first day of the week desperate to hear two-hundred-year-old music written by dead Germans and played on a pipe organ. The audience for music featuring a timpani drum is relatively small when compared to those who listen to the driving beat pounded out on a snare drum. Yet the average American church is far more likely to hire a string or wind ensemble complete with kettle drums than to book a rock band with a full trap set.

This is not intended as a knock on Bach, but rather as a frank realization of the low musical literacy level of our nation. In a similar manner, I am almost always on safe ground in quoting from the latest Hollywood blockbuster, but I am reticent to use any allusion to Shakespeare. Am I saying that the latest Arnold Schwarzenegger character is superior to Hamlet? Certainly not. But far more pew sitters will be familiar with Arnold's dialogue than are acquainted with the machinations of the Danish prince. I may insist on cultural superiority and press forward with unpacking a soliloquy or two. But I may pay a big price of being tuned out by hearers who don't relate to Shakespeare. Obviously, the reason that the works of Shakespeare and Bach have lasted for so many centuries is that they have a superior quality about them. Nevertheless, anything that is not "pop" in a pop culture is consigned to the fringe—perhaps superior to the pop, but unappreciated nonetheless.

While awaiting a delayed flight at the Nashville airport in December 1996, I came upon that day's edition of *The*

Tennessean,[1] a local newspaper. One story, which featured a minister who was retiring after forty-eight years of service, quoted this very committed pastor as saying: "Churches are going to have to move ahead into the *20th* century, which forces a lot of changes" (emphasis mine). It was probably just a simple misprint, but the statement was telling: do we really have to endure *multiple changes* just to move into the *twentieth* century? If so, then what must we do to fit the twenty-first century? I have come to understand that people do not simply *act* different; they really *are* different. Much to my chagrin, my teenage daughter actually likes those terrible-sounding songs on the rock station, and much to her amazement, I actually enjoy listening to talk radio. The twenty-first century is here, and in many ways people are not the same as they were in the middle of the twentieth century. How can we reach them?

What Resonates with Your Soul?

Human beings in all times and places desire to hear the music that resonates inside their own souls, music containing rhythms and harmonies that seem familiar, even when the song is brand-new to them. Thus, Methodism's founders, John and Charles Wesley, set Christian lyrics to popular tunes of their (eighteenth-century) day. Stamps and Baxter wrote revival hymns to music that was fitted to the sounds of the early part of the twentieth century; Carmichael and Peterson followed suit in the middle decades of the twentieth century; and a host of composers have penned hymns and choruses in recent years. Yet most Christian churches, especially those of historic denominational origins, are trapped in a hymnody emanating from another generation and another century.

Lake Highlands Church has a clientele for the old-style music. We have a full house on mornings when our combined choirs are joined by a brass and string orchestra to perform Rutter's *Requiem* or Handel's *Messiah*. But we are also surrounded by thousands of others in our community who are not thus inspired. For generations, American churches have held covered-dish dinners to which each family brought something different to eat. Everyone then had options from which to choose the delicacies they most preferred. Today the need is for covered-dish *services*, to provide options from which people of different sensibilities may choose. Let me be clear: it is, of course, only the style that is different (whether music or liturgy or methodology of preaching); the content forever remains "pure gospel."

We made a conscious decision in 1995 not simply to add "contemporary" elements to our existing services, offering something for everyone. We believed that such a strategy would simply make everyone equally unhappy. Likewise, we did not want to destroy our base; after all, we have a rather sizable contingency of members who vote weekly with their feet that they like our traditional worship experience. Therefore, we elected to offer an alternative worship service for those who are not attracted to the great old hymns and liturgies of the church.

One additional insight supported our decision to add an additional service rather than attempt to reinvent our present offerings: *The easiest way to bring about change is to not require anyone to change.*[2] That is, had we tampered with the existing order, we would have forced many otherwise good-hearted folks out of their comfort zones, creating a backlash against the whole venture. Had we attempted to (a) re-create one of the two already existing services or (b) merely add contemporary elements to one or the other of these services, we would have created hostility and risked losing support and momentum. In truth, to do either of these is to violate the very principle we are trying to give expression to: the people who attend the traditional service do so because it resonates with them.

To take it away or to alter it dramatically is to deny that they have a right to the form of worship that is meaningful to them. Sensitivity must be practiced in both directions. It only makes sense, therefore, to create new opportunities for those who want something different and to see to it that the traditional services continue to provide a meaningful, quality worship experience for those who like that form.

I wish that I could say that everyone in Lake Highlands Church is fully on board with the establishment of alternative worship experiences, or at least be able to say that no one is opposed. But such is not the case. I have one very vocal critic of the contemporary service. He is afraid, he says, that we will dilute the gospel with our new-style music. Although I have attempted to reason with this man, reminding him that once upon a time our so-called traditional service was new, he either cannot or will not hear me. I believe that his own phraseology is correct: he is indeed "afraid." Hopefully his attitude will change as he sees more and more persons like the thirty-something woman who recently professed Jesus Christ as her Savior and Lord. Baptismal waters commingled with the tears of joy running down her cheeks as the meaning of life came into focus for the first time. She and her family first attended our contemporary service when friends who are members of our church invited her. The friends knew the contemporary flavor would be attractive to her, and thus the invitation. Ironically, however, they do not normally attend at 9:44 but instead go to the traditional services; thus, they brought this new family only once. But our new believer and her family were indeed "hooked" on their first visit and came faithfully for several months, despite the fact that their friends did not attend with them anymore. The age-old gospel was presented to this unchurched family in rhythms and harmonies that resonated with who they are, and life transformation was the end product. This story is being repeated week after week as God is at work in our growing contemporary worship experience.

Music Leadership Is Crucial

The addition of a contemporary worship service is impossible without supportive, competent, hard-working musicians. If the music director is not sympathetic, even enthusiastic, then implementing a contemporary service will be extremely difficult. Why would a church musician not be interested? Four reasons: instituting a new service with contemporary music is challenging, threatening, confusing, and stressful for the director. Among the challenges is to find all the key elements for such a service, such as instrumentalists, singers, and the music itself. Contemporary worship may also threaten the music director's comfort zone because it diverges from the kind of education normally secured by even the best church musicians. Excellent classical training does not automatically assure competence in playing pop rhythms. The music director must embrace new musical styles, new instruments, and new technologies. Electronic keyboards with MIDI interfaces are not generally found in even the most progressive seminary program. All the while, the congregation must be scoured for saxophonists, guitarists, and bass players, bringing a world of confusion to the music director's job. Sometimes there are literally no other music directors in the area who can serve as mentors or even as peers because everyone else is doing only traditional worship. Finally, instituting this contemporary worship is extremely stressful for the music director. Juggling all the musicians and extra rehearsals, selecting and learning new music, actually leading "yet another service," all combine to multiply the workload and to make the musician's life more difficult. It is imperative that music directors in such circumstances be committed to the larger vision. If they lose their enthusiasm, the contemporary service may self-destruct.

Clothes Make the Man

Every Sunday, in every city, town, village, and hamlet in America, this question must be answered, "What should I wear to church this morning?" This question is even more complicated for me as the pastor to three different congregations that are all housed in the same building. "What should I wear this morning?" must be answered in three different ways because we have three unique services each Sunday morning.

(1) This service "suits" me. Our early service is especially well attended by older persons, many of whom have rural or small-town roots. A significant and growing number of younger families have been attracted there as well, especially ones with younger children who do not seem to adjust their wake-up time by the calendar; young children seldom sleep in just because it is the weekend. Since they are awake early anyway, and since there are numerous family activities with which to fill their Sunday afternoons, some of these families like to get a jump on the day by attending early worship. In addition, on Sundays when the local professional football team plays the early game of the day, we also experience an increased attendance at the 8:30 A.M. service.

The feel that we strive for in our early service is one that might be found in a strong, traditional church in a small town or even in a rural congregation. Almost everyone is friendly, and the style is fairly relaxed. Although the liturgy is moderately formal, there is an easy air about the service. The Sunrise Choir, which leads the music, sings somewhat easier anthems than its counterpart at 11:00, and often does spirituals. Because the auditorium is only half full, we conduct the service from the floor rather than the platform, so that the minister is close to the people. In keeping with the feel of the early service, I wear a suit.

(2) Full regalia: robe and hood. The 11:00 A.M. service is by far the most formal that we offer each week. Choral introits and benedictions, handbell anthems, multiple choral offerings, sometimes with orchestral accompaniment—all these and more are features of our very traditional, somewhat liturgical, "prime-time" worship hour.

The feel is formal, though not stuffy. For example, we build a time into the service for people to interact with each other. Humor is always a part of this service, primarily because I tend to see the funny side of almost everything. I encourage people to laugh with me and frequently at my foibles. Such a spirit is contagious. Recently, as our associate pastor was preparing for the "Call to Worship," he stated to the congregation in a very deadpan voice that there was a typo in the worship bulletin that morning. Our secretary, he explained, had been ill that week and somehow the typo made it past the proofreaders. "It should read," he stated, "O *Sacred* Head Now Wounded." The associate pastor did not read the misprint to the congregation; he just stood there. One at a time, a few worshipers turned to investigate the misprint for themselves. Scattered chuckles across the room encouraged others to investigate the error for themselves. Soon the whole sanctuary was awash in laughter as people read, "O *Scared* Head Now Wounded." In a truly formal, high-church setting, no such announcement would have been made. Additionally, the congregation itself would have censored its own response such that the laughter would not have occurred. We are formal at 11:00 A.M., though not truly high-church. And because the service is formal, I wear my most formal attire: a clerical robe, adorned with a full doctoral hood. My early service suit would simply be out of place.

(3) Snag my sweater, please. Our 9:44 contemporary service is wholly different from the other two. In addition to
the music I have already described, other elements combine to give it a laid-back, free-flowing form. There are no
formal liturgies other than the Lord's Prayer, which is
printed in the bulletin. The bulletin's primary purpose,
however, is to provide the words to the songs. Some
"experts" suggest that worshipers do not sing as well looking down at a bulletin as they do looking up at a screen, but
we are convinced that this is the best method for us at this
time. We have chosen the printed page rather than projection for two reasons. First, practically speaking, our room is
too light to make such projection truly readable. Without
substantial modifications to our facility or substantial
investment in quality equipment, we think that such projections would render an amateurish, distracting ambiance
to the service. Second, we believe it is helpful to send the
lyrics home with our worshipers, who then can sing and
worship in private all week long. When our sanctuary renovation is complete, perhaps we will install state-of-the-art
LCD display panels, but for now, we will continue to print
our lyrics. Of course, we have purchased the right to print
these songs; we pay a modest annual royalty for the privilege through CCLI.[3] It is only ethical to pay for the right to
benefit from the labors of Christian songwriters.

The contemporary service is built thematically. Every element in it is designed to further develop the theme, until the
call to action is issued, commensurate with the theme, at the
conclusion of the service. Contemporary drama is a popular
offering in many of our 9:44 worship experiences. Written in
everyday language, these five-minute (or less) dramas are
designed to propel the worshipers' contemplation of the
theme for the day. For example, one moving piece focused
on a young person who had trouble believing in a loving
God because of the abuse endured from the family, the very
persons who are supposed to love us most. Currently, we

have purchased the rights to various dramas published by the Willow Creek Association[4] and other organizations. Members of the church serve as our actors, ranging in age from seven to seventy.

Periodically, we also have liturgical dance. There was a time when I would have stopped short of this worship element, my own sensibilities finding offense. However, the persons in our community who perform sacred dance do so in extremely discreet, nonsexual ways that have indeed enhanced the worship experience. "Sacred movement," as we usually call it, is practiced sparingly, not more than twice a year. However, when used, it has been extremely effective at communicating the mood of the service. Beyond the pragmatic consideration, there is biblical warrant for its inclusion amongst the people of God: Miriam, the sister of Moses, danced on the Red Sea shore, and "David danced before the LORD with all his might" (2 Sam. 6:14). In David's case, his wife Michal was outraged because he stripped down to his linen ephod (read: underwear). Scandalous! I probably would have been on Michal's side. But God seems to have approved of his joyful display, despite my wounded sensibilities. Thus, we are willing from time to time to embrace even sacred movement.

Every presentation of the Christian message, whether a sermon, a Sunday school lesson, or any other, must decide the question, "Will you go from Bible-to-life or from life-to-Bible?" to which I answer with a hearty, "Yes!" I am willing to go either way, depending upon the need of the moment. This, of course, is heresy to my classical seminary training that taught me that expository preaching is the only way to proclaim the Word. And for those who know the Bible already or for those who are seeking to learn the contents and applications of the Scriptures, I concur; expositing the Word is probably the best strategy in such cases. But for those who do not know the Bible or are not sure whether it has any relevance to their lives, I am more likely to preach or teach thematically, moving from the issue under discussion to its application in Scripture. Telling stories in response to the felt needs of the hearers, stories garnered from the everyday world of the hearers, has pretty good precedent; after all, that was the primary preaching/teaching strategy of a Galilean carpenter long ago and far away.

Our contemporary service is designed to reach new generations, particularly those who are not yet well-grounded in the faith. It is for this reason that I unashamedly allow a moving piece of music to control the theme of the preaching on that day. Likewise, if we find a powerful drama on, say, a theme of "the ambiguities of life," I may challenge my biblical understanding until I come up with answers to this troubling issue. Most of the people who come to this service do not ask what the meaning of the Bible is, as we might ideally desire. Rather, they want to know if their own lives have any meaning at all. "How can I stand the rejection I feel from my kids?" they ask, or "How can I bear another empty Christmas?" or "How can I continue in a dead-end relationship?" They do not start with the Bible but with the anxiety and pain and perplexity they feel. My job is to take them, along with their problems, to the answers that God's Word offers.

Of course there is a danger that I may preach something other than the Word of God. I may become so lost in my listener's troubles and problems that I may miss hearing what God says. The answers I give may not be what the Bible declares at all. That is the danger of topical, thematic preaching. On the other hand, if I only do expository preaching, I may still miss what the Scripture actually means (even expository preachers are fallible). Yet even worse, the answers I give may not address the issues that my listeners are so overwhelmed by. As Harry Emerson Fosdick said to my predecessor generation, "No one has ever asked me, 'Now what ever happened to the

Jebusites?'" People hurt and want the answers to life. We must avoid giving stones when children beg for bread.

Although the contemporary service appears relaxed and informal, planning for it is incredibly complex and time-consuming. It actually takes more time than the other two services combined. Our music minister, Dale Daniels, and I sit down together with others on the team, attempting to strategize several months in advance. Each brings to the table items that we think could be useful elements for a service sometime: a song, a drama, a sacred movement, a biblical text, or a life issue. With much prayer we assemble the elements that will eventually become several different worship experiences. Just as surely as we plan to use a Bach concerto at 11:00 one Sunday morning, we also plan "Reggae Sunday" at 9:44, a Sunday with a Caribbean flavor and a joyful, exuberant spirit, complete with flowery shirts and dark glasses worn by the the band. We do not always bring off our plans (the lead character in a three-person drama may turn up sick on the Sunday slated for its presentation), but our leaders are all flexible. Somehow, despite the obstacles, the Spirit of God makes things come out in a way that is glorifying to God, and we are ever amazed.

When we started the service, I instructed the music director not to recruit any high school youths to sing in the "praise team" (the group leading the singing) or play in the band. The single exception was Dale's son, David, who at seventeen was already such an accomplished musician that he added something really amazing with his bass guitar. The reason behind my edict was that I did not want this service to be identified as the "teenage service." Certainly we would seek to reach some high schoolers through our contemporary music and laid-back style, but our scope was broader than youth. I feared that we might reach a youth audience but miss the larger community we sought. We have been very successful, and today we have a spectrum of ages, including a seventy-five-year-old couple who attend weekly. Since the service was established, I have relented from my initial proscription. Today, of the dozen or so leaders on the platform, three and sometimes four of them are high schoolers, including one or more of my own daughters.

Because the contemporary service is intended to convey that "this is a safe environment to bring yourself, just as you are," we strive for a relaxed atmosphere. For this reason, I discard my tie and don a sweater. Our conception of this service is perhaps typified best by the set of five Burma Shave-like signs we placed sequentially alongside the major road fronting our property. They read, respectively:

> Cool music—folks in jeans
> A whole casual scene.
> God's Word—no bore
> Starts at 9:44.
> Join us this Sunday!

On most Sundays, the sermon for the 9:44 service is completely different from the one presented at 8:30 and 11:00 A.M. This is because we are addressing different topics since the audience is largely unchurched. Likewise, the style differs somewhat; it is more relaxed and informal. An unanticipated benefit of preaching different sermons at the diverse services is that up to two dozen persons regularly attend two worship services on the same morning. These are folks who, for one reason or another, are disinterested in Sunday school and therefore have no natural vehicle for social interaction. However, by staying around for both hours, they not only benefit from participating in two different worship experiences, they also find themselves socializing with others who are in the same place waiting for the same event to occur. Although this is not an ideal strategy to advance fellowship opportunities, a small step forward has begun.

No *Lite Church*

There is an old joke about the "Lite Church." In the Lite Church there are only eight commandments—your choice. The Lite Church is the home of the 6 percent tithe. The Lite Church demands that you only like your enemies, not love them. For us, a contemporary service is not synonymous with a "lite" service; we are not developing a Lite Church. Although its form of worship differs from other services, the goals remain the same, whatever time we meet or style we embody. We seek to instill the Christian faith in worshipers. We seek to assimilate them into the larger Body of Christ, urging church membership, encouraging Sunday school attendance, and inviting participation in outreach ministries. We teach contemporary worshipers to be good stewards of the grace of God in their lives—to give of their time, talents, and treasures to the Lord. Yes, we make an announcement preceding the offering each week: "We are about to pass an offering plate this morning. This is the way our church members pay for the utilities and provide the facilities that we gather in. But if you are visiting with us today, please know that you are considered to be our guest; all we expect of you is that you pass the plate with a smile." However, once new believers join the church through the contemporary setting, we have high expectations that they will give at least equally to their counterparts in the other services. They then become those who pay for the utilities and provide the facilities as an expression of their gratitude to God. Finally, as a natural part of the contemporary worship experience itself, we take special pains to teach our growing congregation, which is comprised mostly of unchurched attenders, why we practice baptism and holy communion. An explanation is virtually demanded when the sacraments are celebrated, since so many there have little previous experience and woefully inadequate understanding. Although the form of our worship is truly contemporary, the eternal gospel is its content.

Clothes make the man? Perhaps not. But clothes definitely signal to people what they can expect in each of our three services. At 8:30, my suit says "modestly formal." At 9:44, the sweater indicates that we are laid-back: "It's okay to party a little!" At 11:00, my liturgical robe speaks of formal, traditional worship. I have become quite a quick-change artist, not only of my clothes but of the way I preach and the way I conduct the service. We seek to reach people who do not merely *act* different but who really *are* different. All people need the good news, no matter what garment it may be wrapped in. Ultimately, we are not in the garment business after all, but in the disciple-making business. And we are willing to "become all things to all people, that [we] might by all means [win] some" (1 Cor. 9:22).

CHAPTER 5

OUTSIDE THE FOUR WALLS

It's 10:45 on a typical Sunday morning. Milling about, anxiously awaiting the arrival of the pastors and the other leaders who have keys to the building are two dozen eager children, along with a handful of adults. This morning several beer cans are found, inside and out, left over from last night's drunken party on the premises. When at last the leaders show up, some of the children chide them for running late, even though it is still ten minutes away from the posted start time. "We want to sing! Can we sing my favorite song this morning?" one bright-eyed eight-year-old pleads. Her choice is both echoed and countered by other exuberant young worshipers. The volume level of the laughter that pervades the morning's ritual is at times unnerving, but the joy is unmistakably real.

When everyone finally arrives, a total of thirty-two worshipers fill the seats for what promises to be an exceptionally meaningful, if also exceptionally wiggly, morning worship service. Half of the attenders are African American; another 25 percent are of Hispanic origin; and the remainder, including the leadership, are all Anglo. Some of the children engage in a sort of competition to see who can add the most details to the corporate account of yesterday's police raid. A twenty-two-year-old gang leader was arrested and carted away in handcuffs. It seems to be the perfect backdrop to the morning's Sunday school lesson that teaches the children where true fellowship is found—not in gangs, but in the community of faith. For a couple of the younger, first-time visitors in the congregation that morning, it is the first alternative that they have ever encountered to the all-pervasive "gangsta" culture in which they are being raised. Eagerly, they soak up the notion of a community based on love rather than on power and fear and violence. It is more than a concept, however, because here is "Miss Debra" and "Big Keith," as the children refer to two of the many leaders assembled that morning, and each of these devoted volunteers is hugging and caring for them in the tenderest fashion, not rebuffing, not abusing them as so often happens in their community.

This scene is repeated in a number of locations every Sunday when Lake Highlands United Methodist Church assembles for worship. In fact, the above setting was not in our church building at all, but in the "community room" at a large apartment complex located in our neighborhood. Lake Highlands now conducts worship services and a host of other ministries on multiple sites away from our main campus, going to where the people are.

Not Many Apartment Dwellers in Church

By far, the largest and hardest-to-reach group of unchurched persons in this country is comprised of those who live in apartment complexes. American apartment dwellers represent some 30 million households, one out of every three and one-half families in the country. Yet despite their large numbers, surveys indicate that somewhere between 80 and 95 percent of apartment dwellers (depending on the location) are totally unchurched, and their number is growing. This is a staggering statistic. Plainly stated, most churchgoers are homeowners, whereas most apartment dwellers are simply absent from the community of faith.

Those who live in apartments are not all the same kinds

of people. For example, many college students and young adults live in an apartment for a brief time; however, this is an interim stage, and they will eventually move into their own homes when their careers and families are established. Second, people on the other end of the life cycle also move into apartments, those who have raised their families and finished their careers but who now want to downsize their lives and their home responsibilities (for example, lawn care). Both of these groups are more likely to attend church at rates similar to their counterparts in single-family homes. This is in marked contrast to the third group of apartment dwellers who form the bulk of this community. The largest segment of this third group is poor. Most will never fulfill the American dream of home ownership. Socioeconomically, they tend to be lower-middle-class or below. Many are new immigrants in my part of the world, from Mexico or other south-of-the-border countries. Many speak little, if any, English. Although the majority of poorer apartment residents are Anglo, a large contingency is African American. A higher than the national average number of the families in apartments are headed by a single parent. Clearly, this is a "needy" group, but one that is very different from the membership of the average local church.

Many efforts to reach into the apartment community have been made over the years by my denomination and by others, yet without much success. We mail out flyers; we conduct surveys; we do service projects (giving away food, clothing, school supplies, Christmas toys, and so forth) within apartment complexes. We go out of our way to invite "those people" to come to "our church," but without much success. Clearly, a new approach is needed.

The "Key Church" Strategy

Prior to becoming the pastor at Lake Highlands, I served as the church extension officer for the North Texas

Conference. In that capacity, I linked up with my counterparts in other denominations. One of those was a remarkable visionary named J. V. Thomas of the Baptist General Convention of Texas. Several years earlier he had pioneered a new form of church planting through the efforts of a local church in Fort Worth, Texas. The strategy that emerged is now known as the "Key Church," whereby an individual local church sets itself the task of planting numerous new congregations annually.[1]

The ultimate goal of the Key Church, one which we adopted for our Off-Campus Ministries, is to plant new congregations that are self-governing, self-financing, self-expressing, and self-propagating. We do this especially among the poorer elements of society. Although some large, independent churches are planted through a Key Church, most new congregations they launch form in storefronts or warehouses or apartment buildings, anywhere there are underserved groups of people. This is an especially acute problem among apartment dwellers, many of whom are also new immigrants and frequently are poor. The question, of course, is, "How can a large, upper-middle-class Anglo church plant new congregations among poor folks who may be racially diverse and may not even speak the same language?" The basic thrust of our Off-Campus Ministries is directed toward apartment complexes within our community, where we seek to create new congregations.[2]

What will we have if we are successful? A new, active, worshiping community is the answer, with every piece of the definition being important. Our goal is to create something new and active, not merely an extension of ourselves. Likewise, it is insufficient that the new body be just a social group or an organization of those who assemble to get their social welfare needs met. Although such needs are legitimately a concern of the new body, they are not the main concern. Worship is essential, and until worship is going, our efforts are inadequate. But worship is not the end of the matter either. We are building a community—people who know and care for each other, those who assist each other on a spiritual journey. Will each new congregation be completely independent from the "mother" church? Perhaps, but not necessarily so. One apartment complex in which we work is made up of 90 percent senior citizens; this congregation will probably never be fully independent, which is just fine because it can still be an active, worshiping community. What we steadfastly refuse to do is to burden our new congregations with unrealistic expectations that could never be realized through the resources of that particular community. For example, a new congregation formed in a poor apartment community will likely never own its own church building; therefore, we will not go out and rent a facility that we would then expect the new congregation to take over at some point in the future. Our plan is both low-tech and low-dollar. It thrives on a highly labor-intensive strategy. Volunteers come initially from our church membership; eventually, we hope that the workers will come from within the apartment communities themselves.

The Apartment Manager Is Key

The biggest initial obstacle to starting a new congregation in an apartment complex is the opposition of the manager at the complex. She[3] may be wary of outsiders coming onto her turf and starting turmoil on her property. Why should an apartment manager let our church solicit residents? Our initial approach, assuming that the manager does not already know about the kind of work we are doing, is to talk about "something good for everyone." A condensed form of a typical opening conversation might go something like this:

Hi. I'm Richard Dunagin from Lake Highlands Church, down on Plano Road. I would like to talk to you today about an opportunity that we have to help each other out. Let me explain. At my church, we have a lot of members. Part of being a member at our church is the desire to help people—everyone is encouraged to do some good things for others. Now, truthfully, we have a whole lot of members, but only a limited number of things that need doing around the church. So, we are always looking for places to share with other people. That's why we're coming to you today.

Forgive me if I'm wrong, but I suspect that you probably have some problems here. If you're like the typical apartment manager in our area, your turnover rates are a bit higher than you wish, and your maintenance costs are out of sight. And part of the reason for that is that your residents, because they don't know each other too well, don't have much of a commitment to this place. Now, if that's true, I have a suggestion for you.

Our church members, who are looking for some good things to do, would like to offer to come and help you like this: We would come in and offer several different activities for your residents free of charge. We've got members who have all kinds of skills that they can bring—everything from "English as a Second Language" training to "Survival Auto-Maintenance for the Single Female." We can provide children's activities to keep the kids rounded up and doing something constructive for awhile, and we can teach some job skills to some of your residents. And of course, we'll offer Bible study for those who want it.

Now, if you let us come in here, everybody wins. That is, we get someplace to do good things, your residents get a great number of free activities that they can't get anyplace else, and you get something, too. You see, what will happen is this: as your residents get together in these activities, they will get to know and trust one another. As we both know, even though people live right next door, most of the time they don't know their neighbors. Well, they will get to know each other when they're side by side learning English or how to operate a computer or studying the Bible. And as they get to know each other, they won't want to leave their friends, so your turnover rates should begin to decline. Beyond that, since they will be staying, and because they begin to think of this place as "home," they are more likely to take care of the complex. So, your maintenance costs should also go down.

This is our proposal. What do you think? Oh, yes, I have a list of references. Perhaps you know the Brookshire Apartments over on Audelia? We have been working over there for two years. And there is Newport Landing, and Audelia Manor, too.

An apartment manager is understandably wary at first. She faces an overwhelming challenge. She is constantly under pressure to make a profit for the owner, yet she has few resources to do so successfully. There is a high turnover among apartment managers, and those that survive must develop a thick skin. Often, she must serve as a referee and a bill collector, a janitorial specialist and a family-court judge. She may have to evict residents whom she likes and retain others whom she detests. An apartment manager is looking for help, but knows that most offers are disingenuous. But if someone can really help, an apartment manager can be the most receptive person in the world.[4]

Once our ministry has been accepted, we have been treated with the greatest of generosity by our apartment managers. They give us free access to their community rooms. In one instance, our workers are so trusted by the manager that they have their own keys and can come and go at any hours they please to provide any programming they choose. That manager has also given to the ministry on her premises a copy machine of their own in order to make their work more efficient. Other churches report that their managers have given free apartments to their workers, something that we have not felt the need to request up to this point.

Reaching Apartment Residents

Once we have secured permission from the manager, we attempt to survey the residents' needs. Listed on the survey form are many possible activities; we have volunteers who could lead each of these. Sometimes we conduct surveys door-to-door; others are sent out by the management; whereas still others are secured at a "cultivative event." Such events are actually big parties for residents and volunteers to mix and mingle together. Often held in conjunction with a holiday (Christmas, Easter, Thanksgiving, Fourth of July, Cinco de Mayo, and so on), "cultivative events" are excellent tools for meeting new people and winning their trust. We continue to sponsor "cultivative events" at holiday times even after a ministry is well-founded because it still affords us an unparalleled opportunity to connect with additional residents in a non-threatening environment.

At one Christmas party, our youth volunteers staged a live Nativity scene in the upstairs portion of the apartment complex's community room. They escorted the resident children up the stairs individually and allowed them to dress up in a costume for the Nativity scene. Among the wonderful assortment of shepherds and wise men who climbed the stairs that day was a four-year-old boy who announced that he wanted to be the baby (the one getting all the attention—something he missed at home). After lying in the manger for a few minutes while the little "volunteer" baby Jesus from our church took a much-needed feeding break, one of our workers explained the story of Jesus' birth to this beautiful child, who had never heard such a wonderful account in all his brief life. His eyes lit up when he was told that because of the baby Jesus, he too was very much loved by Jesus and by these volunteers.

It takes time to become familiar to the residents. In the initial phases of a new ministry, we must put a lot of effort into building genuine relationships. In order for our own volunteers to understand this dynamic, we use the descriptive phrase, "hanging out on the property," because that is exactly what is required. Off-Campus Ministries offers no quick fix but invites us to invest countless hours just "hanging out on the property." This is followed by weeks and months of showering personal attention on precious, but standoffish, individuals. We are successful in building a ministry only when our volunteers give themselves away in consistent, loving care. We warn our ministry team members that they will invest hundreds of hours in people to whom they otherwise would not even give the time of day. But we also encourage them, reassuring them that the rewards that come because of faithfulness are unbelievable. Because the residents that we deal with are usually in the lower socioeconomic strata, they tend not to be very trusting initially. But if we are consistent, we can win lifelong friendships with the most loyal people on earth.

Children are usually the easiest to reach; thus, the children's program is almost always the first part of the ministry to "gel," although even the younger crowd can be difficult to connect with. In some cases it literally takes years to backfill with a viable adult ministry. One apartment resident, an African American girl of six or seven, was conversing recently with a young volunteer, an Anglo child (also six or seven) who goes each week with her parents to work in an apartment community. The resident child said, "I like you; you're different. People of your color are not usually very nice." We thank God for all such breakthroughs. Whether spoken or not, distrust is a serious obstacle that can only be surmounted by loving individuals "hanging out on the property" over a long period of time.

The Volunteers

Within one year of developing Off-Campus Ministries, we had over one hundred active volunteers to share the work. We believe that the more people we can involve in this ministry, the better the work will go and the stronger the church will become. This is because no other ministry that we perform strikes as close to the heart of the basic mission of the church (to make disciples for Jesus Christ) as this one. All four elements of the primary task are found here: (1) reach out and receive new persons, (2) relate them to God, (3) nurture them in the faith, and (4) send them out in mission. Whatever his or her individual contribution to the overall ministry, each volunteer receives the immediate gratification of completing some piece in the larger puzzle—whether it is conducting an "English as a Second Language" class or bringing cookies for a "cultivative event." Our leaders are generous with their praise for all manner of tasks performed. And when a new congregation is actually established, everyone who participated in its development can feel the pride of accomplishment in something that is of ultimate significance. So many other ministries within the local church do not have such a straight-line cause and effect relationship between the actions of a volunteer and the outcome of new disciples being brought into the family of God. In such a microcosm, all volunteers get a powerful demonstration of how their own particular spiritual gifts are needed for the whole Body of Christ to function properly, a very important piece of learning.

Initial Obstacles

United Methodists and other mainline Christians are generally not very good at evangelism. As much as I wish this were untrue, two decades of declining membership in my denomination prove the validity of my statement. Although every congregation in which I have served as pastor has grown during my tenure, it has not been without considerable work; thus, when I learned of the off-campus model, I realized that it was not as natural a fit for a United Methodist setting as for other, more aggressively evangelistic churches. For this reason, the strategy I pursued in implementing off-campus ministries included a long-term reorientation of our church culture.

Methodists have a historical connection with evangelism. Springing from the soil of colonial America, the new denomination grew to be the largest Protestant church in the U.S. by the 1950s and 1960s. Then, for a variety of reasons, the growth collapsed. Perhaps the single most influential cause of our decline was the misguided notion that "we already have enough churches." Most of these, unfortunately, were located in rural America—where the people were leaving. United Methodism was left with thousands of declining churches located in every small town and open space in the country, while the population was increasingly urban and suburban. What efforts we did make in church planting were fairly well rewarded, such that now most of our largest churches are ones that have been started in the last thirty years, but their numbers are woefully inadequate to meet the needs of a diverse and mobile population. Recapturing the missionary zeal of early Methodism is essential if we are to succeed at off-campus ministries.

In addition to denominational trends, one additional obstacle had to be overcome—the prejudice of our own members. The invited guest speaker at a service club in our community one morning in 1995 was our city council representative. The representative spoke about the issues most important to our community, everything from airport expansion to repairing potholes on city streets. However, the number-one item on this elected official's agenda, "by far," was to "close down as many of those awful apartment complexes as I possibly can, using all the authority of the city at my disposal." The apartments were depicted as the source of most of our neighborhood's crime, truancy, and a host of other social ills. Indeed, police statistics were quoted in order to back up the assertions that were leveled. The speech that morning was not original; it could have been made by a number of the members of my congregation. A great deal of fear and animosity existed between the home-owners and the "apartment people." What our folks, most of whom are homeowners, fail to realize is that the apart-ment community is comprised of real people who are very much like themselves. Although generally poorer, most have moved into this neighborhood with the same hopes and dreams for a better life (especially for their children) that we have. Our neighborhood looks good to them pre-cisely because it is stable and has an excellent school sys-tem—an island of hope for the next generation away from some of the difficulties in other parts of our city. To institute off-campus ministries, our members had to overcome a great deal of fear, for many were literally afraid for their personal safety should they ever set foot on the grounds of an apartment complex. Beyond this, they had to develop eyes to see real human beings staring back at them from the other side of an apartment door. They would have to learn to love these neighbors, whom they now feared, just as they loved themselves.

Getting Started

The first thing I did at Lake Highlands was to begin to introduce the challenge of having unreached peoples in our own neighborhood. Those with ties to the school were especially sensitive to the growing presence of lower- and working-class residents in our midst, since that is the one place where the differences show up most readily. PTA officers are keenly aware of the changing world. A number of families in our area already send their children to private schools in an effort to avoid the disciplinary and academic problems they believe are drowning public education in such a mixed setting. And most of our members could see the demographic changes that were occurring just by visiting the local grocery stores, where people who are obviously lower on the socioeconomic spectrum as well as those who speak different languages are to be found not merely at the checker's stand, but also in the aisles as fellow shoppers.

Our congregation for a long time had attempted to do good works *for* "those people." We have offered an after-school program for low-income families for a number of years. Likewise, several of our members volunteer as tutors at local elementary schools, usually working with children of lower-income families. We provide Christmas toys to indigent families every year. Our members actively participate in the Women's League, the Exchange Club, and dozens of other organizations that work on behalf of families who are lower on the socioeconomic scale.

What was missing, I asserted to our church leaders, was an organized effort to give the best gift of all—the gift of life. Yes, we were doing good, but were we offering God? It was on such a theme that I introduced my congregation to off-campus ministries. If we can provide bread to hungry folks (and we should), why could we not also provide the "Bread of Life" to them at the same time? No, they will never come here, but that does not end our obligation under Christ. We must go to them, but with something more than an excellent social ministry. Yes, we must provide first-class social ministries, but these become a means to a more important end: to win persons to faith in Jesus Christ and to active integration into a congregation of faith that will preserve those new disciples. And since such congregations do not exist, we must create them.

Our Administrative Council decided that we must appoint a task force to consider off-campus ministries. The chairperson allowed me to name the members to the task force. Knowing that the concept was so totally foreign to our church, I selected as the task force chairperson Pamela Clark, a woman who I believed would have both the gifts and grit to actually run the ministry. Pam was eventually hired as our first Off-Campus Ministries director. She demonstrates an immense love for people that is contagious, and she holds a keen appreciation for those who are poor. In order to acclimate the task force, I sent them on a field trip to Mission Arlington, the off-campus ministry of First Baptist Church of Arlington, Texas. Tilly Bergen, their director, is a caring and visionary leader, who is at the same time both wise and simple. Miss Tilly, as she is known far and wide, has built Mission Arlington from the ground up. On any given Sunday, at the last count I had, some fourteen hundred worshipers attend services at First Baptist's main campus. However, in excess of eighteen hundred others also worship in two hundred off-campus settings. Miss Tilly has become somewhat of a mentor to many leaders of similar programs, including our own Pamela Clark. Their visit to Mission Arlington engendered a hunger in the hearts of the task force members.

The task force was charged to bring back an actual plan that could be implemented by Lake Highlands Church to establish such a ministry in our community. They were to include time lines, flowcharts, and financial requirements. I counseled Pam to build a three-tiered proposal—a low-cost model that would barely suffice, a full-bore model that would instantly put us in a league with First Baptist, and a median-way model that would be the most likely for us to achieve. I believed that because the concept was so foreign to us, we would need time to grow in our understanding before we would be good at off-campus ministries. Even if we invested enormous funds and hired a full-time staff for the program, we could not short-circuit the learning curve that we must inevitably follow. Our downside was not finance, but an inadequate institutional culture. We would have to learn to evangelize as well as gear all other aspects of this new ministry to the prime directive—planting new congregations.

The danger in tackling any new endeavor is simply practicing what one already knows. If we did what came "naturally," our church members would do the tutoring and party aspects of the ministry, but we would hire a seminary student to provide all of the spiritual input. This is manifestly not what off-campus ministries is all about. Certainly our goal is to establish a worshiping congregation in an apartment setting, but one whose leadership is not a "hired gun" bought by outsiders. Instead, leadership begins with lay members of our church who, if successful, will raise up lay leaders from within the new worshiping community. Thus, if we were to hire an outsider, especially at a salary rate that the apartment residents themselves could never afford to pay, then we would have: (1) limited the number of works that we can create to the number that Lake Highlands Church can afford (How cheaply will seminary students work?), (2) deprived the new congregation of the dignity of self-sufficiency (Will they never be free to determine their own destiny?), and (3) restricted our church's members to exercising only a select few of their own spiritual gifts, thus depriving them of the joy of real service in Christ's name.

Because we had to transform the culture of our church, I understood well that our time frame for establishing new congregations would be expanded. I sometimes like to contrast our church with a hypothetical "First Southern Baptist

Congregation of Lake Highlands." There, the members have heard all their lives that evangelism is the major reason that Christians are left on the planet. They have always been taught "the plan of salvation" and how to administer some version or another of the "four spiritual laws." Thus, were they to recruit more than one hundred volunteers, First Southern Baptist Congregation of Lake Highlands would likely launch ten new congregations in its first year, whereas we were able to develop only one worshiping community by the end of our first year, plus begin activities at a second site. (Incidentally, I know from my Southern Baptist friends that my fictitious firebrand church starter is more than romanticized. They tell me that if they got a hundred volunteers, seventy-five would bail out the first month, either because they felt guilty for not really wanting to do evangelism or because they decided to start a new splinter congregation of their own.) Nevertheless, the notion of creating a new congregation out of strangers with whom one must first share the evangelistic message is a bit extreme for most mainline Protestants, to be sure. Thus, we have gone at the whole venture slowly and deliberately.

In order to assist our work, we hired as consultant a Baptist minister who has served as the director of a highly successful off-campus program. His primary job with us was twofold: (1) to help reify this radical new concept with our people, training the initial cadre of volunteers and encouraging them in their efforts as well as assisting our newly formed Off-Campus Ministries Board to establish its policies; and (2) to serve as a mentor to our fledgling director. The first task was completed within three or four months; the second continued throughout the first year. We knew that we needed expert help, and we were certainly not going to allow the fact that he was not of our denomination to deter us. In addition, others in that denomination who do similar work have generously welcomed Pam into their network. She has gone to their training events and profited from her continuing associations, having been accepted now as a valued peer.

Results

The main focus for us, of course, is not that we got started with off-campus ministries, but that we are achieving results. These have come in at least four areas.

(1) We have established four active worshiping communities. In some ways, this may sound like more than it is. Yes, every Sunday, at four different locations separate and apart from our main church facility, worship services are held. In truth, however, the largest constituency at three of the four are children. It is far easier to reach kids than it is to reach their parents. But we are discovering that if we are faithful in loving those children and consistently holding the door open for the adults, eventually the parents will follow. Sometimes it is difficult to wait, although our experience assures us that we will be rewarded if we persevere. At one of our sites, all of the residents are adults, most are senior citizens. All are poor. Yet surprisingly, establishing a worshiping congregation there has been very easy. Many residents in that facility have some history in church, unlike their younger counterparts in the other complexes we serve. The average worship service at each of our new congregations includes approximately twenty-five to thirty-five attenders. Our first "official convert" did not come forward for two years; however, on the second Sunday in September 1997, we received our first two church members, who made a formal profession of their faith. One had been baptized as a child many years earlier. The other, a teenager, was baptized in our sanctuary that morning. Our congregation responded with applause—an action that is anything but routine in our normally staid eleven o'clock worship service.

What is happening however, is more than worship. Just as we promise the apartment manager in the beginning of each ministry, a true community is forming. At a recent prayer time, a mother requested prayer because she did not have enough food to last the entire week for her children and herself. While the circle of workers and residents continued to pray about this and other matters, another resident slipped out, only to return just as the prayer time was ending. Her arms were loaded with groceries from her own pantry, which she now freely delivered to her needy neighbor—opened boxes of cereal and crackers, a few canned goods, whatever she had. Although struggling herself, she was unwilling to let her newfound sister in Christ suffer when she still had "more than I need." (Is this any different from the first believers, who held everything in common because they truly loved each other?) The next day, our volunteers supplemented this generosity with an additional five bags of groceries, but their gifts were certainly of no more value than that which was given by this caring resident. We are establishing active worshiping *communities.*

(2) Lake Highlands Church members are proud of Off-Campus Ministries. A healthy sense of pride (I hope it is the godly variety) wells up within our members as they tell others about Off-Campus Ministries. I have heard many skeptical words about our ministry (people wondering if we could pull it off), but not one word of criticism. No other ministry in our church enjoys such widespread support. At the same time, no one in our church would be satisfied were we to stop at four locations; expansion is favored by all. One way to gauge the popularity of a program is to look at how easy it is to pay for. Funding for Off-Campus Ministries is achieved outside of the regular budget, and we have never lacked the necessary monies. In fact, this is the easiest money I raise, a feat accomplished

through a single solicitation letter each year, mailed to only a handful of members. If a congregation is to be proud of something it accomplishes, this is the kind of ministry that I want our members to celebrate!

(3) Lake Highlands Church is developing an excellent reputation within our community because of this outreach. Although our director has intentionally held a low profile for our ministry (e.g., declining newspaper interviews), people in the larger Lake Highlands community are hearing about us. Pamela is often invited to share our story at local civic clubs. Other churches call, requesting "how-to" information and expressing admiration for the work.[5] Our new city council representative asked for a meeting with us to discuss what we are doing to make an impact on the apartment community because he had heard through the grapevine that we were making a difference. And additional apartment managers are calling to request that our volunteers come to their locations. We are finding that this kind of ministry is attractive to spiritually minded newcomers to the community because, as they say, "Here is a church that's making a difference." It also translates favorably to secular people, in marked contrast to the stereotype by which the church is often unfairly judged. Like it or not, many of those outside the church think that all churches are hypocritical, taking from people rather than giving. We do not engage in Off-Campus Ministries for its public relations impact, but that is a nice side benefit. We have also been joined in our efforts by the local Kroger grocery store. Initially they agreed to provide us with free snacks every Saturday morning from their stocks of outdated, but still edible, foods. That provision has grown into a weekly donation of 300 to 500 pounds of food each Saturday. Some is consumed during our children's Bible Clubs; much of it is distributed within the apartment communities; and the rest is taken to our local community food room. Our

volunteers who do the delivery at both places have a keen sense of making a difference.

(4) Our members now care about apartment dwellers. Perhaps the most important effect of Off-Campus Ministries is the transformation it is making in our own people. Whereas our folks formerly feared their neighbors in the apartments, now they genuinely care—at least our volunteers care, if not everyone in the church. The same story has been retold by scores of our people: "We thought we were going over there to give something to them, but we are the ones who have been blessed the most." One of the harder experiences our volunteers have encountered concerned a five-year-old boy who regularly attended Bible Club. A quiet child, he slowly began to warm up to our workers. At some point, however, he was missed, having been absent for several weeks in a row. The workers inquired about him, only to discover that this precious child had died from a blow to the head, perpetrated by his mother's boyfriend. So young, so innocent. The ministry team reviewed photographs taken of the community by our photographer. In several pictures, that small child can be seen up in someone's lap where he is being held and hugged, touched and loved by people who came to that community to serve as the hands and feet of Jesus. Real love is sometimes painful, and the depth of care that signals the change of heart by our people could be seen in the grief they felt for a "throwaway" child, whom they had come to know as one of God's lambs.

One of our volunteers described the ill feelings she previously held toward the apartment community by declaring that she had actually wanted to build a "big brick wall" behind her house in order to separate her property from the apartments. However, through many wonderful experiences as an Off-Campus Ministries volunteer, she now sees herself as tearing down the (invisible) walls that separate them. Many members of Lake Highlands United Methodist Church have undergone a radical reconversion to that "first love" that Jesus calls us all to renew.

In summary, Off-Campus Ministries is working—revolutionizing our community, both inside our church and out. It is successful because it has a clear vision that is fully congruent with the central thrust of the New Testament and because numerous people within our congregation have made it their own. The Kingdom comes slowly, sometimes imperceptibly. But it comes.

CHAPTER 6

THIS IS MY STORY, THIS IS MY SONG

In 1968, Virgil St. Claire was leading an oil exploration venture off the western coast of Alaska. Steaming north in the Bering Sea on the *Arctic Explorer*, one day Virgil realized that he would need to make a side trip to Anchorage in order to consult with company officials. The question was, "How do I get there?" Searching the World War II–vintage charts and maps aboard the ship, Virgil discovered that an Indian fishing village must be close by. He could board a skiff and hitch a ride from the village while the ship continued to steam northward.

Alone on the ocean, guided by his charts, Virgil set out. After some time, he landed. Much to his horror, now far too distant to return to the ship and without radio or much other equipment, Virgil discovered that his map was correct about the location of the village. What it did not tell him, however, was that the village had been abandoned. There was great irony: the setting was the most beautiful he could imagine, but he was truly alone, lost in one of the most isolated locations on earth, a region inhabited mostly by dangerous Kodiak bears.

What do you do when you're lost and alone in a vast wilderness? Strangely, Virgil did not feel panic. He did not grow anxious about his plight. Rather, strangely, wondrously, his mind went back to his boyhood days. As a child, he remembered, his mother loved to sing in the church choir. Lost in this frozen wasteland, her beautiful soprano voice now echoed in his mind. There were two great hymns in particular that he remembered her singing over and over again, not only at church but also around the house. Those two were "Standing on the Promises of God" and "Blessed Assurance, Jesus Is Mine." These great hymns of the faith now gave Virgil a strange sense of peace in the midst of that vast wilderness.

Like Virgil, we sometimes find ourselves wondering how we can possibly survive when we suddenly discover that we are lost and alone in a vast wilderness.

Connecting with the Disconnected

Imagine now that you are sitting in a worship service in your church, and the minister begins his sermon with the story I have just related. Imagine further that the pastor concludes by revealing that the person described in the story is sitting in the pew right there with you that morning, and what is more, that his name is: (you fill in the blank with the name of one of your church's members). That is exactly what I was able to do in February 1997. The real Virgil St. Claire is a wonderful Christian gentleman and a member of my church. I got that story from him, along with his permission to use it in a sermon (as well as in this book). Although a great story in itself, Virgil's account is an even more powerful lead-in to a sermon on "remembrance" that culminated in receiving the communion elements as we "remembered Christ's death." But how much more powerful such a story is when the central character is part of the congregation hearing it!

Lake Highlands is a somewhat large church, with an average Sunday morning attendance in excess of six hundred youth and adults (on our main campus), plus an additional fifty to seventy-five children who are in the building but not counted in worship. It is easy to get lost in such a crowd. The anonymity that is so typical of urban settings has bled over into the church. How do we bridge the gap, especially for those who simply *will not* be folded into a small group, who *will not* join a Sunday school class, who *will not* be assimilated? It is relatively easy for worship attenders to come to feel a bond with the minister who stands before the congregation and shares the Word each week, especially if that preacher makes occasional self-revelatory statements. But the minister's dilemma is this: How can we help our members become more attached to each other, not just to me?

Getting Our Straight Story

During the Lenten season of 1997, I preached a sermon series entitled, "This Is My Story, This Is My Song." During four weeks prior to the Lenten season, I asked, cajoled, pleaded, and shamelessly begged the congregation for personal stories of God's activity in their lives. For two weeks running, we included a bulletin insert on Sunday morning—a 5½-by-8-inch paper titled "This Is My Story, This Is My Song," on which worshipers were invited to share their own experiences with God, whether joyful or sad about God's guidance, God's mercy, God's answer to prayer, God's correction in their lives, God's support in tough times, or any other interaction with God. For those who shared an anecdote, I also invited them to request a hymn that goes with their story, or they might simply suggest their favorite hymn. I promised the church that if they would tell me of their encounters with God, I would give voice to their witness. Since most of us are not public speakers, this was a way that each could witness to his or her faith in a broad arena.

Already, I anticipated that the stories would cluster around certain themes:

- God answers prayer
- God guides through his providence (Incidentally, I cryptically named that one "You Don't Have to Go to Rhode Island")
- God brings victory out of tragedy
- God comforts us in sorrow
- God redeems us

Many Lake Highlands people responded; I received some fifty stories. Indeed, they did address the themes that I anticipated, plus a few others as well. I was struck by the honesty of these stories; several divulged deep, often quite painful, chapters of their lives. Although I offered the option of keeping their experiences anonymous, I said that I needed to know who wrote each narrative. My stated reason was that I might require clarification, or perhaps legibility might be a problem. The other (unstated) reason in the back of my mind was that I did not want some prankster turning in false stories—the kind of mischief that I might have engaged in when I was a boy. Although I stated flatly that I might not actually use every story in a sermon, my intention was to do so if I possibly could. In some cases, I lumped similar anecdotes that were sparsely detailed into a generalization, merely mentioning, for example, that Person A has experienced many answered prayers, as have Persons B and C. The more detailed account of Person D was then used in the body of the sermon.

The Risk of Being Too Personal

Such a venture is fraught with risks. The first of these has to do with creating a feeling of violation in those whose personal stories are revealed. Although church members may grant their permission to detail their lives, they may feel exposed and embarrassed afterward. (Incidentally, many pastors who have done deeply personal counseling know this phenomenon: following fruitful in-depth counseling, all too often the counseled parties will leave the church. They may have revealed too much to ever feel comfortable in "normal" interaction again. The pastor knows all of their innermost "secrets," and that can be quite disconcerting.) A great deal of discretion is required while telling of the drug abuse that Eddie's son wrestles with. Likewise, when Fred details his promiscuity, it may not be wise to name him.

Two principles guided my decisions about how to proceed. (1) First, as a general rule, *we ought not to confess other people's sins.* Thus, if Eddie (hypothetical name) tells of God's helping in his struggle with drug abuse, it is appropriate (with Eddie's permission) to use that account in a sermon on God's help with our weak and sinful flesh. On the other hand, if Eddie's account is of the trials he has encountered in handling his son's drug abuse, I would deem it improper to divulge Eddie's name because to do so would hold the son up to other people's scrutiny. (2) The second principle under which I operated was this: *One must balance the sensitivity of the self-revelation with the level of one's personal acquaintance with the teller.* That is, if stories were quite intimate and I did not know the tellers well, I was less inclined to reveal their names. For example, I received an anecdote from a woman about her endurance of spousal abuse in a former marriage. The particular situation is one in which the offending party, who would remain unnamed in any event, would never be known to the congregation; thus, general rule number one was not particularly germane. The question naturally arises: Would her sense of personal dignity be violated by revealing this part of her past? That is not a question that I could answer unless I already had a fairly thorough acquaintance with her. In this instance, since I did not know her well enough to answer the question, the only reasonable course was to share her story anonymously. If she chooses then to reveal at a later date that she is the person in the story, that is her decision. On the other hand, I felt perfectly free to attach names to a touching account of God's tenderness encountered by a family when their daughter was diagnosed with schizophrenia. I was free in this case because I know the family well and know that they openly and often speak of the situation. Likewise, their wonderful daughter is well-known and loved by the congregation.

A second set of issues must also be faced when we tell our own stories. Do we not run the risk of preaching our-selves and not preaching Christ? Of course we do. But I would suggest that such a risk is not unique to homegrown sermon illustrations. The test for the legitimacy of any particular story is this: "If I had read this story in some other publication and the person in it was a stranger to me, would I use it to make my sermon come alive?" Ministers often tell tales for personal aggrandizement and not to glorify Christ; the problem is not the story's source, but the speaker's use of it. I was determined not simply to string together several "great tales" as a sort of verbal Lake Highlands travelogue, but to preach the Word of God. God alone is a good judge of how well I succeeded, but my best assessment is that I did about as well as I normally do in that regard.

The Three Results

What was truly unique was how these sermons were received. Many congregational members have urged me to publish the entire sermon series, swelling my pride. Others have asked that I publish just the stories themselves, bringing me back down to earth. One member told me that he had been instructed by his neighbor to "take notes on *our* stories," since she was extremely ill and could not make it to church that day. A woman with a frown on her face lamented that she had missed the previous three Sundays:

"I had no idea that it was going to be so good! I'll be back every week from now on," she promised. "This Is My Story, This Is My Song" has become the all-time favorite sermon series I have ever preached. More tape recordings of these services, as well as written copies of the sermons, have been requested than of any others.

(1) Making a connection. Throughout the series, church members continued to come to me, declaring, "I have a story, preacher. I'm sorry I waited so long to write it up for you. Is it too late?" Many of these were among the leaders of the congregation, yet many others were on the fringes, persons who were not at all integrated into the fabric of the church, including some regular "visitors," who have not yet taken vows of Christian commitment in this congregation. "This Is My Story, This Is My Song" became in fact their conduit into the larger arena. For the first time, in many instances, some folks were able to make a contribution to their church, and they felt "connected." This is particularly significant for those who would otherwise resist intimate involvement. No longer were they confronted by an anonymous crowd called "the church." We were becoming a true community.

(2) Congratulations, you're normal. A second effect of the sermon series is that it began to normalize Christian experience. Some of our congregation, who themselves had encountered God in a powerful and deeply personal manner, had half believed that they were the only ones to do so, much as Elijah thought himself to be the only true believer left in his day. As a result, many of our folks seldom verbalized their experience of God. In classic Christian terms, they were reluctant to "witness." Suddenly, we no longer conceived of ourselves as isolated believers, experiencing our own private epiphanies with the holy; instead, we were in a spiritual community that could actually expect God to

intervene in human affairs, since this was a regular occurrence among the people of God. We could now see our spiritual lives differently:

> It is neither strange nor abnormal to experience God's providential care.
> Christ leads his flock; I know, he has led Sandra and Suzanne and Jim.
> We ought not to lose heart in prayer: God does use prayer in working out the affairs of women and men; just ask Betty and John.
> We are not wrong to look for victories, even in the bleakest of circumstances. Larry and Don can attest to it, and so can I!

"In other words," as one young person put it to me, "this spiritual stuff works!"

(3) We're alike after all. A third, and not dissimilar, outcome is that our congregation's members began to see each other as fellow disciples. Rather than encountering other church members as (a) problems to be solved ("How can I get him to vote for my pet project at the next Board meeting?") or (b) functions to be fulfilled ("Now, let's see, she is the chair of the missions commission, so I must address her in this way."), we began to see each other as real people. "This Is My Story, This Is My Song" became *our* story and *our* song, with a heavy emphasis on *our*. When I related one woman's near suicide that followed her abandonment by her husband, not a dry eye was found in the congregation, and many other women were able to share their anguish at marital breakup. A story of wrestling over whether or not to adopt a baby whose birth mother had been a dope user brought a new compassion for those who are unable to conceive. And an account of God's sustaining a mother through the death of her child helped a number of similarly situated parents who had carried such scars for years.

Even more important, the underlying message became: "We are all in this together; we are all fellow sufferers. Who knows what is going on in the life of the person in the next pew? Perhaps her story is like mine. Maybe we can help each other along." Many barriers were broken down.

My plan is to revisit "This Is My Story, This Is My Song" periodically in days to come, though not necessarily as a full-blown preaching series. I completed the series with a number of excellent tales still untold, which simply awaited a more fitting setting. Perhaps best of all, members of the congregation now feel free to bring me accounts of their latest experiences with God. They know that if they are willing to divulge them to me, I am willing to spread the word abroad, for this indeed is our story, this is our song. God is alive and well in our midst.

CHAPTER 7

BUILDING FOR
THE TWENTY-FIRST CENTURY

Everybody likes a birthday party. And special birthdays ought to be observed as milestones in life's journey. These two notions led, without any particular intentionality in the beginning, to a rather dramatic outcome for our church.

Lake Highlands Church was founded in 1956; thus, as we approached 1996, we began to design a fortieth anniversary celebration. In planning meetings I noted that forty years seems to mark a generation in the Bible. We therefore played with a theme that would highlight a generational transition combined with our new understanding of our disciple-making mission. It seemed only natural when the fortieth anniversary theme, "Reaching New Generations for Christ," was adopted.

We anticipated holding multiple events spread throughout the year rather than simply one big celebration day. First up: we scheduled Ken McIntosh, our founding pastor, to preach in January. We hoped to cap the celebration off with a visit from our new bishop in November. The fortieth anniversary planning team quite innocently began to ask about a birthday present: "It's a party; don't we need to give a present to the *next generation?*" Their logic was impeccable, but what *could* we give; what *should* we give? We talked about various programs we might design to reach new generations, but in truth we were doing all the new programs we could sustain at the moment. Besides, a "lasting" gift seemed more appropriate, something concrete (or something "brick and mortar," if a pun is allowed). Thoughts naturally turned to renovating our church plant.

Our Church Plant

The physical plant of Lake Highlands Church was built in four phases during our forty years. The oldest part, constructed in 1956, is now used for church office space, classrooms, and the fellowship hall. The second phase was our children's building, which was constructed just a couple of years later and still serves in that capacity. The sanctuary, complete with classrooms and choir space in its basement, was constructed in the mid-1970s. The final addition to the complex was the family life building, which houses nine large classrooms, an oversized gymnasium, a refreshment center, and a modest commercial kitchen, all built in the mid-1980s. The sanctuary was updated once in the early 1980s, but even that did not stop a chronic roof leak, which was caused by the large mounts to the tall, narrow cross attached to the top of our pyramid-shaped edifice. That vast roof has leaked from virtually the day of its completion in the mid-1970s all the way through the mid-1990s, despite repeated attempts to correct the defect. By 1996, the whole complex was in decline. Funds had been lacking to fully care for its maintenance during a number of years.

In recent days we had begun a remodeling project on the hallway of our administrative wing and in the fellowship hall. It was delightful to see the renovation, for the deterioration there was severe: floor tiles did not match; multiple, oddly shaped bulletin boards lined the paint-peeling walls; exposed burglar alarm wires combined with multiple phone lines and miscellaneous electrical wires rendered a haphazard and unattractive appearance overhead. And perhaps worst of all, the lighting was woefully inadequate.

The hallway that led to our offices was thoroughly uninviting. But as happens so often in the church, those who had been here the longest did not see the problem. Unfortunately, worshipers headed for the contemporary service must travel through this eyesore to enter the fellowship hall where the service is conducted. Alas, that room, too, was dilapidated and dark. The floor was the original, 1956 vintage, and very much used. By pooling funds raised by various groups in the church, we were able to transform this whole area into an attractive and inviting facility. Yes, it was delightful to see this critical need being addressed. But these projects were already in the works, so what next? What permanent addition to the building might we consider as a fitting birthday present?

From Small Tower to Total Renovation

Fact: The leaky sanctuary roof was a long-standing source of embarrassment. On a rainy Sunday morning, an unsuspecting visitor might find herself "baptized" without ever walking to the front of the sanctuary. With such a problem as this, when the fortieth anniversary planning team came up with the idea to remove the cross from the sanctuary roof and place it instead on a separate, to-be-constructed tower, people applauded. According to several engineers, this would allow a permanent repair of the roof, replacing the problem roof fixture with an aesthetically attractive symbol of the faith. With a projected cost of perhaps $30,000, this seemed both doable and appropriate. When the chairperson announced the concept, there was a slight tone of regret in his voice. "I actually wish we could remodel the whole sanctuary; that's our real need. But we have to face reality; we couldn't possibly do something that huge."

At the subsequent Board of Trustees meeting, the tower concept was discussed. Everyone agreed that this would make a fine birthday gift. But soon the wistful speech of the chairperson was echoed by all of the members of the board, as they talked of large-scale sanctuary remodeling. Many long-standing deficiencies were detailed. Our sanctuary was designed by an architect who had a keen theological sensibility. Unfortunately, from my perspective, the architect spent too much time on theological symbolism and too little on architectural practicalities.

The sanctuary is built on a trinitarian theme: it actually has three sides, not four. Additionally, on the floor in front of the platform sits a large, three-sided communion table, enclosed on all three sides by an expansive communion rail, complete with kneeling pads. Rather than lining the front of the platform as do communion rails in most United Methodist Church buildings, our sanctuary features this large, prominent, and unusual stand-alone structure in the middle of the worship center. What is thereby created, however, is not symbolism, but a chasm between pastor and people, interposed as it is between the front rows of the two middle pew sections and the platform. Such a barrier makes it difficult for the pastor to truly "connect" with the people.

Another unusual feature of the building is that the choir, organ, and piano are located at the back of the room, behind the people, not on the front platform. The architect's theory was that the congregation's focus on God alone should not be broken by the presence of musicians. Their music is to be heard as a sort of anonymous offering to God, not as a performance to be observed. Of course, logical person that I am, I found myself rather indelicately asking why we don't then use recorded music. Wouldn't that be more "anonymous"? It is also unclear why the preacher is not also a distraction, who should therefore be consigned to the rear as well. This rear choir loft is not in a true balcony, however. It is only slightly elevated, a fact that tempts many worshipers to turn around to watch when the choir is singing. However, the line of sight from pew to choir loft forces the worshiper's gaze directly through the person seated behind, creating a most uncomfortable situation if that person does not also turn around. And if the discomfort of violating someone else's space is too great and the worshiper relents by turning back to the front, those in the row just ahead are just as likely to be turned around also. Discomfort is almost inescapable, it seems.

In addition to these deficiencies, the sanctuary is dark, without natural lighting; the artificial lighting we do have is likewise inadequate. The building suffers acoustically as well, as it is virtually without reverberation; singing is often unrewarding to individual worshipers, who hear themselves overmuch. Our sanctuary also has no center aisle due to the blockade created by the central communion setup, a fact that is seldom lost on would-be brides. Even more crucial, little gathering space is available, with tiny twin foyers, one each on two sides of the sanctuary. This severely limits the ability of congregants to fellowship with each other before or after services. Too often, visitors perceive our church as unfriendly, when the real issue is that literally no space exists in which to demonstrate our friendliness. To stand in the foyer to chat is to invite "death by stampede" as other worshipers walk out the door. A final deficit of the sanctuary is its inaccessibility. One must travel out-of-doors in order to move from the rest of the complex into the sanctuary, except for a single indoor entrance through the gym into the sanctuary basement, then up a steep flight of stairs. Until 1996 there were no ramps into the sanctuary; wheelchair-bound persons were literally picked up (wheelchair and all) and carried into the building.

In light of all our deficiencies, the Trustees asked themselves in 1996, "Why can't we go for a larger amount? Why can't we give a lasting gift that is really in keeping with our goal of reaching new generations for Christ?" I could think of at least 900,000 reasons why we could not; that was the amount of our indebtedness, which has been a source of grave concern for quite some time. In fact, for ten of the eleven years that preceded my arrival, Lake Highlands Church had failed to achieve its budget. During those years, the surplus building funds that had been left from the previous capital campaign had declined precipitously until they were virtually negligible. In effect, we had been eating up our life savings for many years. How could we possibly raise a bundle of extra cash sufficient for this new cause? Yes, we had met our budget in 1994 and in 1995 with money left in the bank, but the years of famine were too recent to feel secure yet.

It is perhaps important to understand where I was, as the church's senior pastor. I knew that a church our size could reasonably raise one third of last year's budget for an attractive one-time cause. The $30,000 tower should be simple to finance if the people liked the concept. Likewise, I knew that we could, if we chose, mount a major capital funds campaign that could net somewhere between one and one-and-a-half times last year's budget. Since we had received some $750,000 in 1995, if we elected to support a capital effort, we might be able to raise $750,000 to $1,125,000. But this all seemed a pipe dream because I had heard the fear and poor-mouthing from day one of my tenure at Lake Highlands. Quite frankly, I did not have faith to believe that this congregation was anywhere near ready to mount a major campaign. I was surprised, perhaps even shocked, to hear the Trustees discuss it seriously. As in virtually all churches, the two most conservative bodies in the administrative structure are the Trustees and the Finance Committee, and this church had shown itself representative, even exemplary, in this generalization. So why would they even talk like this?

It was because of my misreading of the congregational

mood that I played only a minor role in the beginning of the largest capital fund effort in our church's history. The laity took the lead, especially the chairperson of the Trustees, a fifty-year-old attorney with a long tenure in the congregation. The Board of Trustees voted to take the concept to the Administrative Council, who, much to my surprise, appointed the Trustees to explore the possibilities with an architect. In short order, we were seriously discussing an extensive remodeling of the sanctuary, which would cost at least several hundred thousand dollars. When we started talking about raising significant funds, I knew that I must exercise some critical leadership. I immediately made my appeal that we consider hiring an outside firm to run our campaign. This was for three reasons.

Why Hire a Capital Fund-raiser?

(1) A "homegrown" plan is never complete and is always up for review. If no one is an "expert" with the rallying cry, "Here's the way to do it," then a campaign's outline and implementation will always be up for reconsideration. Someone will inevitably have a better way to do things, and since we haven't paid anyone to "come put on this campaign for us," then we are forever rewriting the script and endlessly arguing about how it is to be handled. In contrast, when we hire an outsider, even though we don't like elements of his program, nevertheless, with only minor modifications, we agree that "this is the way we're going" because "this is what we've paid for." I did not want to endure constant disagreement over the campaign itself.

(2) A "homegrown" plan interferes with pastoral functioning. If we develop our own plan, *someone* has to finally author it and put it into action. That someone almost inevitably is the pastor, the only one in the congregation with the time, talent, and clout to implement such an effort.

Such a strategy has two highly undesirable side-effects: First, the pastor who spends his time fund-raising is not spending his time pastoring. The ministry, which this new building is designed to enhance, languishes, calling into question the need for a new building after all. Second, the pastor who spends her time fund-raising changes roles. No longer is she viewed as a pastor, but as a fund-raiser. This is perhaps the most important dynamic behind an often observed phenomenon: frequently, pastors move to another church shortly after the completion of a new building. This is because they change roles, and the congregation becomes unhappy. After the construction is complete, the pastor is either unable or not allowed to shift back to the pastoral role. Feelings are sometimes damaged too greatly. Not wanting to move anytime soon, I highly recommended that we pay the extra money to hire a professional fund-raising organization.

(3) A professionally run campaign usually raises more money. This is true for several reasons: First, with the clarity and focus of a well-designed professional campaign, everyone "gets on the same page." Disputes over methodology are settled. Second, the ministry of the church, especially through the person of the pastor, continues on-target. Third, a professional campaign is usually well-designed; these are "professionals" in the field, after all! Fourth, a good professional fund-raiser can give us realistic feedback on what is truly feasible, both in terms of financial capabilities of our people and in terms of exercising faith. Many of the best companies are run by godly people who have one foot firmly planted in fiscal responsibility and the other in a deep faith.

A Project Too Big?

Without the assistance of an architect or other design professional, we had estimated that we could remodel the sanctuary for some $350,000, all of which we wanted to raise in one year. Even before hiring the leading capital stewardship organization in the country, its president advised us that it would take no more work and very little additional expense to run a three-year campaign rather than a one-year version, yet we could expect to raise approximately three times as much money. What if we could remodel the sanctuary for $350,000 and, at the same time, pay off our entire $900,000 debt? This was not completely out of the realm of possibility. Shortly, the Trustees were recommending to our Administrative Council that we develop just such a plan, which the Council approved.

An architect was soon hired to create some preliminary designs. However, just as the scope of the capital finance campaign had increased, so did the building plan itself. As any good architect would, the man we hired asked what we really wanted and needed. "If you could fix all the problems, what would those be?" We began to tell him our dissatisfaction with our current space and to lament our other deficiencies. And soon he came up with a much expanded design, which addressed all of our concerns. Not only could we remodel our sanctuary, moving the choir and organ to an elevated and expanded platform in the front, but we could even knock out the side walls in order to move the pews outward, thus creating a center aisle; we could add a balcony with one hundred new seats; we could even build a new connector building that would tie our facilities together. Then no one need go outside to move from building to building. Likewise, an elevator could be installed that would make every part of the complex accessible to every person attending. Additionally, on the ground floor of the connector building, we could create a large, comfortable, and attractive gathering space to increase our "friendliness factor." And below, new classrooms could address the problem of our overcrowded Sunday school. Of course, all this increased space came with an inflated price tag. New projections ran between $1.2 and $1.3 million. Adding the current indebtedness even to the most conservative of the architect's estimates ran the total to $2.2 million, a figure I knew was unattainable.

Although the drawings were everything we had hoped for and more, at this point I was quite certain that someone would simply announce that the emperor was once again running around without clothing, and that would be the end of the remodeling. I was, once again, mistaken. Our people had caught a vision. Seldom did they speak about the "pretty new building *we* would get." Rather, the emphasis was on preparing ourselves to reach the next generation for Christ. Our theme thus became "Building for the Twenty-first Century," with a subtitle of "Reaching New Generations for Christ."

There were detractors. Most of these were people who had felt left out of the last campaign, some ten years earlier. During that effort, promises were heard (whether actually made or not is the subject of a long-standing debate) to the effect that no funds would be borrowed to complete the family life building. When the bids came in far higher than anticipated, approvals were sought (and secured, although not everyone remembers those formal meetings) to incur $1.2 million in indebtedness. Some of those who had opposed that process then opposed the new plan now. They feared a repeat of the previous actions that, from their perspective, had saddled the church with unmet budgets that strained our ability to function. No, they said, we cannot incur new debt. It was for this reason that the promise was made by me first, and seconded by both the Board of Trustees and the Administrative Council, that we would not borrow even one dime toward our new construction. Instead, we would operate on a "pay-as-you-go" philosophy. Despite the assurances, some folks remained unconvinced.

Making a Capital Funds Campaign Work

Throughout the summer we prepared for the capital stewardship campaign by selecting committee members. The key to success in any such enterprise is to capture the imaginations of as broad a sweep of the congregation as possible. In many ways we are a very typical mainline congregation. Our membership rolls exceed our average attendance by a factor of three; that is, on average, only about one-third of the congregation is in attendance on any given Sunday. Likewise, our budget is paid by just barely half of the members, with the other half giving nothing all year long. To break it down further along the lines of the old (nonetheless true) adage, 80 percent of the money is given by 20 percent of the members. The key to a successful capital funds campaign is threefold: (1) to get that elite 20 percent to give generously to yet another cause, as they always do; (2) to encourage the next 30 percent (who normally give the other 20 percent of all our funds) to step up their giving for this special cause; and (3) to tap that heretofore "ungenerous" remainder. We must have widespread involvement.

Normally, United Methodist congregations are *very* democratic, and everything runs in a *very* systematic way. However, for this campaign to work, leaders had to be chosen carefully; perhaps the normal protocols would be unsuitable because different qualifications for leadership were required. The capital stewardship organization we employed always suggests that the senior pastor select the leadership, which I did, although I also sought counsel from other staff and from lay leaders. This was a special campaign that would last only a few months, and its leadership would be crucial. Eventually, virtually every member of the church would be invited to serve in some capacity or another in a sort of sanctified "pyramid scheme," but we must start with those leaders who would inspire others by their example and their solid commitment to Christ and to Lake Highlands Church. By midsummer the leadership team was selected, and we only awaited the fall for the campaign proper to begin.

Mostly, the "campaign" was a series of training meetings for the multiple layers of participants in the effort. After the top layer of leadership, the jobs were largely routine—from stuffing envelopes to organizing dinner parties. Most of the training could therefore be accomplished in a rather brief time. That allowed for the bulk of each training meeting to be devoted to two essential tasks: (1) sharing the vision of the campaign's outcome, that is, "What we hope to accomplish with the money"; and (2) telling exciting stories of campaigns in other churches that had successful outcomes, that is, "How people in settings much like our own have given sacrificially."

One of the casualties of the capital stewardship effort was the tent revival we had planned in honor of our fortieth anniversary. Our church had never done anything like it before, but the concept had intrigued our members when I first proposed it a year earlier. The goal had been to engage in an evangelistic effort that would reflect the era in which our church was initially planted, the 1950s, the heyday of mass evangelism, especially tent revivals. We planned to erect a tent on our front lawn for a week in late September or early October. We would "soften" what we were doing by parking 1950s vintage cars out front and by having the female and male choir members wear poodle skirts and letter sweaters, respectively. This was a wonderful plan, my own proud brainchild, but one that I personally aborted. I did so because I learned a long time ago that one cannot adopt a new priority without, at the same time, dropping something else. We could not simply add on yet another big activity to an already overpacked fall schedule and do justice to both major undertakings. I knew that either one or the other (or most likely, both) would suffer. The same people would, in many cases, be tapped to run the twin events, and it was likely that many crucial details would simply fall through the cracks. I was unwilling to risk failure because we would not pass this way again anytime soon. The capital effort was too important, and if we failed, we might permanently impair even our own self-conception. The tent revival might have to wait for our fiftieth anniversary.

I wanted everything to be done first-class, from printed materials to Sunday brunch. Everything about the campaign must reflect the importance and seriousness of the effort. First-class and slick are not synonymous, however. This is the church, not Madison Avenue. Our efforts must be excellent, yet understated. Thus, we produced a video to explain the program, a video that technically was incredibly sophisticated, yet still had the feeling of being homemade. Indeed, it was homemade, shot by a fellow pastor who has excellent equipment. I wrote the script and directed the action, while he handled the camera work and other technical elements. The "rough edges" actually enhanced the value of the finished product, from my perspective.

The capital stewardship consultant who led our effort offered an excellent blend of knowledge and challenge. He told heartwarming stories of other churches (mostly United Methodist, including several that I knew), yet he did so without any sense of manipulation. The worst possible scenario is to have the congregation primed to give but then turned off by a manipulative salesman-type fundraiser. Although not a United Methodist himself, our consultant was very attuned to our culture and did an excellent job of inspiring us.

One example of his flexibility came when it was time to establish campaign goals. In most capital funds efforts, three goals are set: (1) a low level that virtually assures the church's attainment of "success"; (2) an intermediate level that the leaders privately hope they will attain; and (3) a super level that is highly unlikely, but one that occasionally churches rise to. As is his duty, Jim submitted to me in advance the goals he planned to present to the steering committee for us to adopt. They were perfectly rational goals, ones I might well have established on my own; nevertheless, the problem virtually jumped off the page as I first laid eyes upon the numbers. We had advertised that we needed $2.2 million to build our buildings, remodel our sanctuary, and pay off our debt, and that $1.2 million was the minimum for the construction effort alone. And yet, here were three goals that all failed to do the job, two of which even fell short of this "minimum" number. How could I tell the congregation that we could be happy with either of the lower two numbers when neither allowed us to do the job? Why, even the highest of the three was woefully short of the amount called for in order to accomplish the whole program. It would be only reasonable for folks to say to themselves, "See, just as I thought, they planned to borrow money all along. Look, they're not even planning to raise enough to build their buildings. Those preachers are all alike." Most of our members would never think this way, but if I could deduce such chicanery from this report, surely those who were already suspicious might have some reason to be so.

"Hey," I said, calling the consultant on the phone. "We've got a big problem. Although I believe your calculations are excellent, we cannot use these goals." When I explained my dilemma to him, he readily saw my point. All along we had told our people that we did not have a fall-back plan; if we failed to achieve the funds we had suggested that we needed, we would look at that situation when it arose. All we knew was that God was leading us in this direction and we were determined to walk in it. Although we were committed to not borrow any additional monies, we would not conjecture about what else we might do (have another campaign, scale down the project, and so forth) if we failed to achieve the $2.2 million. What we finally elected to do was simply not to adopt any offi-

cial goals, but merely to continue telling the people that
$2.2 million was the need. At the same time, as a reality
check, we reminded everyone in leadership positions of
what had been stated from the beginning, that the average
for a church in our situation is to raise one to one-and-a-
half times last year's budget.

One of the final exercises the consultant led our campaign steering committee to do was to write down two figures on a piece of paper. One was the amount they thought
they might give personally. The other was the amount they
thought the campaign would achieve. (It was actually par-
tially from these figures that Jim developed the aborted
goals.) My own estimate for the campaign was $1.2 million;
I thought I was quite optimistic, though secretly I feared
that the amount would be far less.

We finally came to the completion of our campaign in
November 1996. The actual commitments were taken and
the figure announced on the third Sunday of that month. I
cannot say how flabbergasted I was when the final tally
was $1.8 million. Obviously, this far exceeded my own
wildest expectations. The support was broad and the commitments were sacrificial. This is best seen by the fact that
we failed to conform to the "normal distribution" chart for-
mulated by the capital stewardship organization. Given
their many years of experience, they can calculate a table of
gifts, estimating, for example, how many $10,000 gifts a
campaign of such-and-such a size will generate versus how
many $100,000 gifts it will bring. To achieve $1.8 million, a
church our size should have had a "lead gift" of $200,000.
We did not. Instead, many of our members gave so much
more than would normally be expected that they made up
for the lack of such a lead gift. This was very heartening,
for it bespeaks how committed our people are to the
advancement of our ministry into the twenty-first century.

The first phase of the building project was to replace the
roofs on the administrative building and the fellowship

hall, a feat accomplished in September 1997. As of this writing, the funds are continuing to accumulate in anticipation of eventually completing the project. For obvious reasons, no work will be initiated until all necessary funds are in hand, which should be accomplished by the end of 1999, when Lake Highlands will be building for the twenty-first century.

CHAPTER 8

WHAT KIND OF LEADER AM I?

Many books have been written on leadership in recent years. I have benefited from reading several such works by learning concepts and principles on the one hand and practical tips and concrete strategies on the other. For the purposes of this book, I would like to describe what I believe are the most crucial issues that I as a pastor face in exercising my leadership. Some of my actual practices, as regards staffing, are detailed further in the next chapter. In this chapter I will address the four most important leadership questions that pastors must answer for themselves: (1) "What is my self-understanding, that is, what is my role as a minister of the church?"; (2) "How can I keep my own spiritual life alive?"; (3) "What is my primary task as a minister?"; and (4) "What are the key items that I must take charge of?"

What Is a Pastor?

Perhaps the most crucial question that ministers can ask themselves has to do with the role that they occupy as pastors. We operate within a complex system with at least three competing definitions: (1) we must understand ourselves in some way according to the biblical ideal of "a shepherd who guides God's flock"; (2) we must come to terms with the institutional norms that are presented to us by the complex, historical organizations that we head; and all the while, (3) we must grapple with the shifting winds and new discoveries of modern leadership theory. Although I will only note this last element in passing, there is actually much help available for the minister who is willing to investigate the many books, journals, conferences, and whole organizations that have emerged in recent days to assist ministers in self-understanding and the actual practice of leadership.[1]

The biblical model, of course, defines pastors as spiritual leaders who connect a willing and hungry flock with the Source of life. Our job is to serve as both priest and prophet, spending our days uniting a gracious, outreaching God with needy human beings. During my first pastorate, however, a wise, older minister clued me in. He said wistfully, yet forcefully, "You must never mistake the institutional church for the kingdom of God. They are two different things." And he was right. There is nothing particularly spiritual about much of the daily work that pastors are called upon to perform throughout their ministry. For example, how spiritual is it to lobby the finance committee to get "parking lot re-striping" into next year's budget, or to call the air-conditioner repair crew before Wednesday's choir rehearsal, or to select the color for the flyer that will be mailed tomorrow announcing the upcoming men's breakfast? Alas, all too often there is little reverence even in the pre-meal prayer we're called upon to give at the Lion's Club or any real holiness in the three-minute devotional we present on the front end of a women's service project. Much of what we do as pastors is anything but spiritual. For better or for worse, we run complex institutions that are often bogged down with mundane concerns that can choke the spiritual life out of everyone involved.

Added to the creeping cynicism from knowing that much of what I do is not terribly spiritual is the problem of congregational expectations, which are often very unrealistic. Whereas some would make the pastor a general flunky whose job is mainly to keep the operation running smoothly, others demand that their minister frequently visit in their homes and never miss a hospital call—even without notification that a parishioner is ill. Although many individuals will always carry their own idiosyncratic assumptions about the pastor's role, I believe that the expectations of most congregations can be reoriented. The issue is how pastors present themselves.[2] By design, there are some tasks that I have never learned to perform (for example, how to operate our church's commercial dishwasher). Likewise, I know that I am not gifted with my hands (a gross understatement). I highlight this fact by frequently making myself the butt of jokes about my klutziness, often from the pulpit. Besides being true and making me appear more human than I might otherwise, such honest confessions of my mechanical ineptitude also keep congregational members from expecting me to be Mr. Fix-it, even though some of my predecessors have been cast in that light.

Although I conceive of myself as a shepherd for God's flock, I also know myself to be the chief executive officer of a complex organization. The trick for me is to exercise both roles in such a way that the institution actually furthers the spiritual advancement of those to whom I minister—both inside and outside of the congregation. It is all too easy to lose one's soul in the process of pastoring a local church. For this reason, I have always struggled to retain a spiritual base for my work and not get bogged down in trivial or institutional concerns. In order to stay focused on the fundamental things, I use four strategies.

How a Pastor Can Stay Spiritual

(1) I return to the Scriptures again and again. Although I am not an "up-at-dawn-to-read-the-Bible-for-thirty-

minutes-each-day" person, I do find that frequent devotional reading of the Scriptures is essential. I tend to be a "binge person," one who may not have read the Bible much yesterday or today, but who tomorrow may devour it for two hours. Incidentally, this is in line with my basic personality structure: I am the kind of person who does not eat by the clock or dress by the calendar. Instead, I eat when I get hungry and wear clothing appropriate to the temperature, much to the chagrin of my wife; she eats because the clock tells her that it is "mealtime" and dresses in long sleeves because it is October, even though the temperature is 85 degrees, as often happens in Texas. I study the Scriptures when I have a spiritual hunger. They nourish me, sometimes for a day and sometimes for five, as I continue to digest their contents over an indeterminate time frame. When I'm hungry again, I return to them. Some will see this description of my practice as a confession that ought to be placed in chapter 10, where I deal with some of my failings, but I do not believe that my lifestyle is somehow less Christian than that of my more systematic brothers and sisters in Christ. The psychology of temperament, especially as seen through the Jungian-based work of Myers and Briggs,[3] convinces me that half of all human beings tend to be highly organized and to work well using fixed schedules, but the other half of us are not so inclined. Incidentally, it is the orderly group who tend to write the "how-to" books on leadership and on Christian devotion, books that engender guilt in the other half of us who are not so inclined. Many highly effective people are not so orderly, and many very spiritual persons are "bingers," just like myself. The key for us is to feed ourselves when we are hungry, so that the Word nourishes our souls.

(2) I pray constantly. Just as I preach to others, I must likewise be a consumer of the Christian faith and practice its historic disciplines. Prayer is the ongoing communica-

tion with the Lord who guides me. As most pastors do, I practice many different forms of prayer—from reading someone else's formal printed prayers to virtually hollering at God about my latest crisis. As with the study of Scripture, I have no formula for prayer, except that I find myself longing to connect with the divine. Sometimes I have to leave my office, where the phone constantly rings and an endless stream of people rolls through, in order to find quietness to reconnect with God. The church office can actually be one of the worst places on planet Earth to attempt to encounter God. In a very real sense, I believe that clergy and laity face the exact same struggle to live a godly life in a secular environment. The difference is that most laity recognize their own workplaces as secular, but not their local church office. Prayer, which is the constant servicing of an ongoing relationship, is essential.

(3) *I read sermons.* My purpose here is not to get another illustration for next Sunday's homily, but to hear a word from the Lord for me. Of course, I read the sermons of other preachers and often find great help, but frequently I become sidetracked by the turn of a phrase or by an apt illustration or by the alliteration of the three points, and my soul misses the message. For this reason I often study my own "used" sermons. Throughout my ministry I have nearly always preached to myself, seeking to apply God's answers from the Scriptures to my own deepest needs. Much like the psychologist who enters his profession because he is looking for answers, I have always preached to my own hopes and hurts. It is for this reason that some of the sermons that I read with the most profit are ones that I myself preached years earlier. They are usually well fitted to my condition, for, like most people, I continue to wrestle with the same problems year after year; thus, what I preached in the 1980s is still relevant to me today. Victory comes—but usually more slowly than I would like, and it often seems

appropriate to revisit a topic that I have addressed in a sermon on a prior occasion. And if I have already preached a sermon, my focus remains purely on hearing from God, rather than discovering a great point to use in next week's message, as so often happens to me when reading someone else's work. There is power in the word proclaimed and applied through a sermon. Of course, I would be either an incredible egoist or an abject fool if I only read my own works. I hope that I am neither, and thus I also profit from studying Fosdick and Buttrick, from Willimon to Swindoll. I am an inveterate sermon reader.

(4) I connect with fellow pastors. Weekly, I eat a meal with a group of longtime friends in the ministry. The conversation at these gatherings is wide-ranging—from a heated discussion of the nineteenth century quest for the historical Jesus and its modern equivalent to an impassioned request for prayer for a fellow pastor's straying children. We compare notes on why last week's attendance was lousy and on how to structure next year's stewardship campaign. Some days are intensely personal and deeply spiritual, whereas others are just gripe sessions about the ineptitude of our national church agencies. I have often wished for more intimacy in this fellowship group, but in truth my fellow pastors are about as forthcoming as I am.

Unfortunately, in a system such as ours, ministers are almost always extremely guarded. This goes beyond normal human apprehension about self-disclosure; it is actually a function of our ministerial placement system. "Advancement" to one's next appointment in my denomination is dependent upon the perception of the minister held by the presiding bishop and the district superintendents. If a minister is perceived to be weak or troubled, that person's potential for advancement is thereby diminished. Indeed, such a label may continue long after the initial difficulty has dissipated; thus, "openness" can be tantamount to professional suicide. And yet the human heart craves fellowship; we are made for sharing. It is because of these two contradictory factors that it is both difficult and essential to find a group of fellow strugglers with whom a trusting and open relationship can be forged. Although ministers seldom articulate this dilemma, it is nonetheless real: we are spiritual beings who long to be known, understood, and cared for by another; but we are also locked in a bureaucratic institution that may punish us if we reveal our real selves.

I do not mean to denigrate any individuals who serve in supervisory roles in my own denomination or in any other. My experience is that most of these are fine people; many are deeply spiritual and strive to be pastoral with the ministers under their administration. The problem is not personal, but institutional. There is an inherent conflict between the two major roles that are delineated for any bishop or superintendent in their administration of the personnel under their authority. To be pastoral, they must be supportive and encouraging and forgiving. But to supervise their personnel requires that judgment be brought to bear; hard questions must be answered: "Given what I know about Rev. X and Rev. Y, which one of these two is better suited to be the next pastor at Church A? Rev. X seems like a nice and competent minister, one whom I do not know well on a personal level, but one who has never gotten into any trouble. On the other hand, Rev. Y once confessed to me that he has had problems with [*lust, alcohol, spiritual doubt*—fill in the blank with any number of issues that frail human beings face]." Even if the supervisor personally liked the flawed minister better than the other, duty would perhaps demand that the untainted pastor be appointed. I have, of course, oversimplified this whole process, but I believe that the point is clear. The wise words of that older pastor still ring in my ears: "You must never mistake the institutional church for the kingdom of God. They are two different things." I need fellow pastors to hold me accountable and with whom I can do a little reality-testing. But I have selected my peers, not my supervisors, to fill this role. The test will come when one of us becomes a superintendent.

The Primary Ministerial Task: Setting the Vision

Among the many duties that pastors are called upon to perform, the most important, by far, is setting the church's vision. Someone must answer the identity question for the organization: "Who are we and why are we here?" Like other tasks in the ministerial job description, however, vision-casting cannot be done in isolation. Just as one cannot write sermons if removed from or indifferent to the needs of the particular people to whom one preaches, neither can a minister create a "generic vision" for the church if that minister fails to consider who this particular congregation is as a unique expression of the Body of Christ. The vision emerges through the complex interplay of prayer, experience by the pastor, congregational history, the challenges and opportunities that currently confront the church, the assets that the congregation brings to the work (people, money, facilities, training, and the like), the community setting, the willingness of the congregation to give themselves away, and much more. At some point, however, the pastor is the one who must synthesize all these things into a coherent vision for the church. Should the minister fail to do so, the congregation will drift, perhaps headed in the general direction of some previous pastor's vision, yet "tossed to and fro by every wind."

Just as it is essential to discover who these people are before attempting to lead them in a particular direction, the leader must also devise a pace that is tolerable for the group, going neither too fast nor too slow. An anonymous author once cast this light on leadership's challenge:

> Are you a leader?
> Look behind and see if anyone is following.

He who thinks he is leading
and no one is following
is only taking a walk.[4]

Knowing What to Control

Because people are different, there is no pat answer to the question, "What should the pastor control?" But it is a crucial question that all pastors must resolve for themselves. For example, I have a friend who is the senior minister at one of the five largest United Methodist churches in the country. He says that he is indifferent to programming; he has no need and no desire to determine what programs are used in his church. Those decisions he leaves to other staff and responsible lay leadership. However, he completely controls every aspect of worship, going so far as to allot the various participants time blocks, delineated down to the second. His church has a worship committee with exactly one member—himself. If some musician takes an unauthorized minute to speak a word of introduction to a piece of music that is to be performed during worship, there is a "reckoning" following the service. My friend is clear about what he must be in charge of, and so is his congregation.

Some readers will perhaps be turned-off by the term *control*. I have toyed with other phrases in order to blunt the force of the word. *Take charge of, be responsible for, oversee* are possible substitutes, and each conveys part of the concept to which I am referring. However, whatever euphemism is adopted, the end result is the same. A minister, like any other responsible leader, regardless of the field of endeavor, must finally accept the awesome responsibility for decision making. As I jokingly say to my members, some of whom earn six-figure incomes, "That's what you pay me the big bucks for." I cannot do everything, but there are some things that I must personally attend to.

At Lake Highlands, I carry the title of "pastor-in-charge." Although I take my responsibility seriously, I do not attempt to control everything. For instance, I have turned over our church's youth ministry to Alan Hitt, a highly capable youth minister. His job is to run a program that makes disciples of our teenagers and their families. I trust Alan to do his work well; if I did not, I would not keep him on the staff. Thus, I feel no need to look over his shoulder. However, I do want to be kept informed of major developments: when conflicts arise, I expect to hear it first from Alan, not from some angry parent. Likewise, when he shifted the thrust of our Sunday night youth programming from small groups to an emphasis on worship, I learned of the concept before the decision was made, not afterwards. I oversee Alan's work, but I do not dictate it. I am obligated to debate the relative merits of this or that decision if it is important and I disagree, but it is rare that I would ever tell him that I wanted him to scrap something he has chosen. For the most part, I consider myself to be a supporter of his ministry and a member of his team. Ultimately, of course, I am Alan's supervisor, but I could never be his controller.

For me to function effectively, I need to control four areas of our church's life.

(1) Vision. Already I have stated that casting the vision for the church is the number-one task of the senior pastor. It is equally essential that I exercise vigilance to guard the integrity of the vision. It is not enough to lay out a vision if it subsequently gets watered down, ignored, and even supplanted. Sometimes I find that I have to reject competitors. An example: Our church had recently launched its off-campus ministries. At the same time, I was in the process of developing an overarching vision for a ministry to the whole family (see chapter 11) when a leader in the congregation approached me with a new ministry idea. The program she proposed was excellent in many ways, for it reached into families in crisis by training volunteers

who, under the guidance of a psychologist, would "counsel" children from divorced settings. In evaluating this proposal, I quickly realized that its implementation would require a large number of volunteers from within our church. This would bring the new ministry into direct competition with off-campus ministries, our biggest volunteer user. Beyond this, the proposed program by itself had little spiritual content. Instead, it was more psychologically oriented. As a child who grew up in a divorced home myself, I certainly saw value in the approach, yet I found it inadequate as a program in isolation, when measured against our main mission of making disciples for Jesus Christ. Accordingly, I both surprised and disappointed the proponent when I simply vetoed the idea out of hand. However, I indicated to her that the program had merit and in all likelihood would eventually become a component in our overall family ministry. Within that larger context where the well-being of the whole person (including the spiritual nature) would be addressed, a program that meets the psychological needs of children from divorced settings would be very valuable. But for now the timing was wrong for two reasons: (1) we could not allow volunteers to be siphoned away from off-campus ministries; and (2) we must not adopt programs that are not part of an overall disciple-making thrust. I am grateful for the patience and understanding exercised by this committed layperson. She has been able to work in just such a counseling program through another congregation, and she knows that eventually we will probably incorporate it into our own family ministry. She appreciates what we are trying to do and understands why we had to say no for the present in order to guard our vision. Initiating a vision is important, but meaningless if alternatives thrust it aside. It is my task as pastor to cast the vision, but it is also my duty to implement this vision and protect it for the greater good of the church.

(2) Staff. If I am to be responsible for the overall health of the congregation, I must be free to put together a team with whom I can mesh. Most staff-parish committees with which I have worked have readily seen this principle—an effective team must have some form of internal cohesion, be committed to the same goals, and work together for a common purpose. I must be free to build just such a team.

Although I have always asserted this authority, I have never insisted on eliminating any existing staff. This has been true for at least three reasons. First, I have always believed that I could work with almost anyone—a supposition that has proved true in virtually every case. Second, I dislike telling people that they have failed in their life's chosen path. Such confrontations seem inevitably hurtful, and I shrink back from all such painful experiences. The third, and by far the most important, reason is that although I have the authority to terminate staff, I do not automatically have the power. There is a huge difference between authority and power. For example, a policeman confronting a criminal always has authority, but if the criminal is the one with the drawn gun, the criminal is the one with all the power. Entering a new setting, the newly assigned pastor-in-charge has authority, but a much loved, long-term staff member may in fact have more power. To prematurely fire such a person may cripple or even abort the future ministry of the pastor. For these reasons I have often retained staff members whom I judged to be less effective than others. In such instances I have encouraged incongruent staff members to upgrade their skills for ministry through continuing education and networking with other, more competent peers in other churches.

When new staff are to be hired, I insist on having the final say. When we were replacing our music director during my first year at Lake Highlands, I screened many candidates. Ones that I thought might be acceptable I brought in for an interview, first with me and then with both the staff-parish committee and members of the music program. I would never select someone who was incompatible with our music people; however, I made the qualification that "the person chosen was someone that the senior pastor wanted" number one on our list of selection criteria. This may appear at first glance as controlling in the most negative sense, and of course I have already confessed that staffing is an area that I want to control. However, I am unapologetic, believing that if I have to supervise them, and if I am responsible for final outcomes, then I must have the ability to select my staff. No CEO in any other organization would settle for anything less.

(3) Communication. If the church is to present a consistent face, the communications from the church to its constituents must be consistent. For this reason I feel the need to exercise some control over our church's communications vehicles. I usually give a read-through of the church newspaper, checking for tone as much as for content. For example, finance committees sometimes get "antsy" during the leaner summer months and in November, when they are facing the end of the year. And sometimes those anxious, well-meaning committee members want to insert reminders into the church newspaper to alert the congregation as to our current financial difficulties. All this is appropriate; however, sometimes those articles are written with a tone that suggests panic and impending doom. Now such an approach is appropriate and can even bring about the desired outcome when the crisis is real. But as a routine tactic, it is counterproductive for at least two reasons. First, if members perceive that we are always in a crisis mode, they become weary. Members may well say to themselves: "I give my money to those birds all the time, yet it never seems to do any good; we're broke again, and sinking fast. What's the use?" I might rescue a person who normally is okay but has temporarily gotten into a jam, but I become

immune to the cries of a perpetual whiner. Second, we all like to support winners, not to merely throw our money down an ever-expanding hole. Here a member might well say, "If the help I gave during the last crisis six months ago didn't do the trick and now we're in trouble again, then this must be either a poorly run church whose mismanagement will keep it from ever being successful or it's a dying church. Either way, I want to get out." The better communication strategy is to emphasize the positive: "Things are going great; send more money so we can keep up with the challenges and opportunities that we're facing." I certainly do not read every piece of correspondence that goes out from my church, but I do look at the major items with the largest impact, such as visitor packets, all-church financial letters, our yellow pages ad, and the church newspaper.

(4) Worship. Although not as "fanatical" as my friend cited above, I believe that I must exercise my authority as the pastor-in-charge over the worship services of our church. The services must have some sort of internal coherence. In chapter 4 I described each of the services we currently offer. These are not planned by a committee with its various and sometimes competing interests, often trying to add in something for everyone. Rather, they are planned by a small worship team consisting of the senior pastor and minister of music, with input from the associate pastor and other music staff. I am always open to suggestions from other people, especially our Worship Committee (who handle usher responsibilities, budgeting for music programs, and the like). Still, I reserve the right to make the final decision on what we do or don't do. Incidentally, I have never publicly stated this right/responsibility, but it is such a fundamental self-understanding that no one has ever questioned me about it (which illustrates my point above about one's self-presentation). Sometimes my decisions are not liked by everyone, as when I refused to allow the children's musical to take the place of the 11:00 A.M. worship service, but everyone seems to understand that the call is mine. I feel the responsibility most keenly to provide a worship service that is meaningful to all those who attend and that is glorifying to the God for whom we gather.

In a recent "Geech" cartoon strip, the preacher and a church member, Brother Purvis, are seated next to each other at a lunch counter. The preacher begins the conversation, "So, Brother Purvis, will you be in church tomorrow?"

Brother Purvis responds, "What's tomorrow?"

Preacher: "It's Sunday!"

Bro. Purvis: "Then I'll be there."

Preacher: "Will you be awake?"

Bro. Purvis: "I will be when I get there."[5]

People come to the church more or less interested in hearing from God, more or less seeking to satisfy their spiritual hunger. If we destroy their interest by not speaking God's message, and if we feed them stones rather than the "Bread of Life," the fault is not with those who drop out. The preaching, the prayers, the music, the liturgy, and even the announcements must be high quality and must fit together so that the worshiper has the best possible chance of connecting with the living God. Here, the institutional must take a backseat to the truly spiritual. Providing an alive, consistent, and faithful worship experience is a sacred trust, and just as difficult to guard as the vision. The ultimate responsibility for it rests upon my shoulders; this is the essence of the call to ministry that God issues to would-be pastors. Obviously, some pastors can accomplish this duty through sharing the responsibility with a broader group of people than I do, but I suspect most, if not all, would feel the urgency to "take charge" whenever the basic integrity of the service is threatened. We are, after all, shepherds over God's flock.

CHAPTER 9

ASSEMBLING A "DREAM TEAM" OF YOUR OWN

The church staff controls any church whose average worship attendance eclipses thirty-five. I know that the term controls sounds neither democratic nor spiritual, but on the other hand, it is the right term to describe reality. This is not to denigrate the role of the laity, for indeed, no church can be truly great without great laity. But it is a frank acknowledgment that church leaders, like leaders in all other walks of life, exercise an inordinate influence on their organization.

The senior pastor, obviously, carries the most critical role in the local church structure, but the pastor need not necessarily be a superstar if, instead, the rest of the staff is excellent. The truly essential ingredient is how the team functions *as a team.* An altogether average pastor can still head up a first-rate staff that can yield excellent results. Likewise, an altogether gifted pastor can be undermined by an inept or recalcitrant staff. The ideal, of course, is to secure a first-rate team of superstars, all of whom are willing to blend themselves into a team effort. However, this is an unlikely scenario in the real world for at least two reasons. First, superstars often do not blend themselves into team efforts. Indeed, most people do not, whatever their level of expertise; but it may be especially difficult for one who is exceptionally gifted to harmonize with others, since most of the "others" fall beneath the standards of the superstar. Second, by the very definition of the term, most of us are *average,* which means that most church staff people will not be superstars, but instead will have average abilities. It is therefore unlikely that many church staffs will be composed of an integrated team of superstars.

Obviously, I look for basic competencies to work well in the area of ministry that is under consideration. I ask, "Is this potential music director a gifted musician?" or "Can this budding volunteer coordinator truly connect with potential volunteers?" or "Can this future youth minister relate both to youth and to adult workers?" I do not always look initially beyond certain minimal levels of competence and a basic aptitude needed to do the work, however. This is because I believe that skills can almost always be improved; likewise, teamwork can be learned. What cannot be easily transformed is the basic character of a person. It is for this reason that in choosing new staff members, the first, and by far the most important, characteristic that I consider is the character of the individual under consideration. I would rather hire someone with inferior training who has never worked in a team setting, yet who exhibits a good character, than hire the most renowned superstar. What traits are essential to a good character? In one sense character is one of those things that "you know it when you see it" yet is hard to define. Several aspects to a good character can be delineated, however. I like to frame the character issue with a series of four questions that I ask myself about each staff applicant. I carry on an inner dialogue all the while that I am interviewing candidates for ministry positions in my church, attempting to get a fix on their character.

Questions of Character

The first and most important question I ask is this: "Is this a person who can minister to me personally?" Here I figure that if the answer is not positive, then how can I expect the congregation to respond any differently? I am looking past differing personality types and differing gifts to something of a "spiritual essence" of the person. There are many humble and genuinely nice people in the church world who, nonetheless, lack a sense of spirituality that would enable them to minister. Admittedly, this is the most subjective of my four questions, yet it is the most crucial. I have known staff members who meant well but who just were not particularly spiritual people; they did not elevate my spirit, and I sensed that they could not truly minister to others. Some were people whom I genuinely liked and even had an abiding friendship with, yet they were simply not suited for ministry. When expressing such an evaluation of another human being, I find myself asking, "Who are you to judge others?" The answer, of course, is that I am the senior pastor of the church, whose responsibility is to bring together an excellent team who can advance the work of Christ in and through my local congregation. Someone else will surely be judging my effectiveness as a leader, and one of the areas they will (rightfully) judge me on is how well I choose other staff members. Obviously, this is not an issue in the hiring of some personnel—secretarial or custodial staff, for example—but it is an essential question for anyone on the ministerial or program team. A minister of music who cares only about music and not about relating people to God is just as much a turnoff for me as a minister of evangelism who's looking for new members but knows nothing of the saving work of Christ. What if the director of children's ministries can put on great children's programs, but when asked by an eleven-year-old how to encounter God, can only tell the child to talk to the pastor? In our staff meetings, the director of our preschool is just as likely to lead the devotional as the associate pastor, and her words minister greatly to my soul. I seek people who can minister.

A second and almost as important question that I ask myself about potential staff members is this: "Who is the hero of this person's life?" We all have a sense of self and a sense of pride, but I need to discern whether these are inordinate in our candidates. That is, do the persons under consideration take themselves too seriously or give themselves too much credit for their accomplishments? Although talking about God's ministry, too often applicants fail to mention God at all. It's as if the Almighty were merely sitting on heaven's sidelines as a sort of "ministry groupie" who stands in awe of the candidate's great achievements; God is almost indebted to them for all the good work they have done for the sake of Christ. For some, the word "we" never crosses their lips. Rather, they sound like opera singers warming up: "Me, me, me, me, me, me, me, me, me," they intone.

This is not to say that I look for staff members who have no personal identity or sense of achievement. But I do hope to spot some basic sense of humility, which is both becoming and essential for truly spiritual ministry. Often braggarts are merely covering up their own insecurity; whereas truly accomplished and confident folks have no need to convince others, their works speak for themselves. And if our one true hero is actually Jesus Christ, rather than ourselves, and if we truly "fall in love" with him, then our speech should reflect an inward attitude of gratitude and humility toward him; it ought to come out in an interview. Although there are many "heroes of the faith" enumerated in Scripture and in church history, all of these pale in comparison with Jesus, who, in the words of the apostle Paul, *"is* my life" (see Col. 3:4). This apostle is in fact a model of what I believe is a healthy self-perception. On the one hand, he could tell with gusto what great things he had been involved with, but on the other hand, he could then deny that his own works were anything more than "refuse." For him, the essential thing was not to gain "a righteousness of my own," but "to know Christ and the power of his resurrection" (Phil. 3:9-10).

For many years now it has been fashionable (in mainline circles at least) to shy away from appearing overly spiritual. This seems to be due in large measure to a reaction against religious hucksters on the one hand and against well-meaning, but uneducated, believers on the other. Obviously, no one wants to be numbered amongst religious charlatans, some of whom have been rather rudely exposed in recent times. And for those who consider themselves to be intellectually astute (as all of us mainliners do), it would be demeaning to be classified with the "superstitious" and unsophisticated masses. In the mostly homogeneous and religious American culture of the 1950s, in which almost everyone was a Christian, it was perhaps possible to disdain any display of faith. But the world has significantly changed, and perhaps in part because of this attitude. Today our society is mostly secular. Many Americans have grown up without any Christian influence whatsoever, yet with all the spiritual needs that human beings have always experienced. To shrink back from any outward exhibition of one's spirituality is to blend in, chameleon-like, with the secular majority, but at the same time it is to hide the Bread of Life that is so desperately craved. We do not have that luxury any longer if we are to have any self-respect as "ambassadors for Christ." Let me be clear: Speaking about the church is not the same thing as speaking about Christ. Our faith is called *Christ*ianity rather than *Church*ianity for a reason; the center of our lives is to be the Savior, not the church.

I listen carefully to the speech of potential staff members; do they talk about Christ Jesus, or only the church? I ask the question, "Would you please tell me about your faith heritage?" If their answer is only a rehearsal of the church and not an account of a vital relationship with Christ, then I am wary. We must talk about our faith in a living God, with whom we have a vital relationship. More and more, mainline Christians are reclaiming their more ancient heritage as faithful witnesses who proudly own the name of Christ. Those with true Christian character make Christ the hero of their lives and faithfully and freely minister in his name.

A third question I ask myself about all potential staff members, regardless of position sought, concerns a basic character trait: "Is this person deeply honest?" Clearly, custodians must be honest, refusing to take what does not belong to them. Likewise, a secretary who lies can do a lot of damage. But basic integrity is even more essential for a ministerial or program staff member. Sometimes one must listen very deeply to perceive this trait, or its lack. We must hear what is not said as much as what is stated. All of us tell stories selectively, but what is left out? Is it something that makes us look bad? Something that makes my opponent look good? Am I willing to say "I don't know" or "I was wrong," even when I want to look good to those who are important to me? This is not unrelated to the second question about the hero of my life. The absence of this kind of basic integrity can be a great detriment to the work of the church. For example, an eighteen-month-old toddler "escaped" from the three child-care workers who were working at a special kids program one afternoon. Her grandmother discovered her unattended granddaughter wandering freely on the parking lot and was mortified. Although the three child-care workers responsible for this youngster "sort of knew that one of the kids had gotten out," none had gone outside to look for her when she was lost, and none told the program director that the little girl had escaped, even after the child was found. Several hours later, an angry and shaken mother called the school to ask what had happened. The director was totally in the dark and now doubly embarrassed, both because the incident had occurred and because she hadn't known of it before the mom's call. Those child-care workers lacked basic honesty and will not be employed by the church again, but the damage is already done. Basic honesty is crucial.

A fourth question I ask about potential staff members is this: "Will they be committed to the success of the overall ministry of the church?" Some people are afflicted with tunnel vision, whereby they are able to see only their own individual piece of the church's work. Taken to an extreme, staff members may believe that other ministries in their church are in competition with their own; they act as if they are playing a spiritual version of a zero-sum game. These folks are threatened if they perceive that other staff or other ministries are doing better than they. For example, although choir rehearsals are important, occasionally a rehearsal must be canceled for an all-church function; does this antagonize the music director? Likewise, youth ministry is essential to the church, but what is the youth minister's reaction if another special event requires the youth group to move to a more cramped space for the evening? And how does the children's minister react when a Sunday school teacher decides to reinvest her time in outreach ministries instead of teaching the fourth-graders next semester? This is essentially a question about team spirit. All too often, church staff build their own isolated empires. Ominous signs of this are seen when certain staff members never attend any church program unless they have a direct part to play in that program. Likewise, when there is overlap between ministries, does a problem erupt? For example, how well do the children's minister, the youth director, and the music leaders cooperate on the church's big Christmas or Easter programs? Or on renewal services?

In order to ascertain how well potential employees live such a team spirit, I ask questions about their present and former coworkers. "How did you get along with your coworkers? What were the greatest sources of joy in that setting? What antagonisms did you have? Who on the staff did a great job, and why?" Such questions frequently reveal more about the one answering than they do about the other workers. I also ask about how they helped one another and how they functioned in a team spirit. I have observed firsthand how dysfunctional it is when staff members are in competition with each other, and some even engaged in open conflict. The work of God's kingdom is too important to get bogged down in power struggles. I remind our staff frequently that if one member of the staff is not successful, we have all failed. We are all in this thing together, so how can we make each other successful?

These four questions help me to arrive at some assessment of my candidate's basic character. If they can pass the character test, and assuming they have average or above-average intelligence, staff members can always learn new skills and develop new ministries. Indeed, all of us must learn new things—from word processing to Internet usage—just to keep conversant with the changing world. But again, it is far easier to make an impact on the minds of future staff than to change their hearts. If they are not people of character, we are in deep trouble.

Hiring from Without Versus Hiring from Within

In recent years a trend has emerged, especially in the larger program churches, to hire new staff from within the ranks of the church's existing membership rather than seeking an outside expert to bring into the congregation. In general, I applaud the trend with only a few reservations.

(1) No acculturation needed. The most important advantage of hiring from within is that the new staff member already knows and, theoretically at least, is in tune with the "culture" of the church. That is, every congregation functions differently from every other—who does what, who

has what authority, how folks around here see the world, and the like. Likewise, each has its own set of values and mission emphases. For some, overseas missions are crucial, whereas for others, the great sacred cow is the high quality of the classical music program. Those who have been intimately involved in a congregation over a period of time absorb its culture and values, and in fact probably share them personally because they have continued to choose that congregation for themselves. An "outsider," on the other hand, probably has developed a different reality set, having lived in a different cultural milieu. Obviously, human beings can adapt to new settings, but the issue is in doubt at the beginning; and sometimes even though expatriates relocate physically, emotionally they may never do so. With a "homegrown" staff member, not only is the issue never in doubt, neither is there any lag time necessary for acculturation.

(2) You know us. A second, and rather obvious, advantage of hiring from within is that the new staff member already knows the people, not only culturally, but individually. Learning names and relationships, the character of individual groups, which members are faithful and which are "flaky," takes a great deal of time. When newly hired employees are already church members, they can devote their full attention to engaging in the work. They do not have to ask if John Q. Member is one who keeps his volunteer commitments or if Jane Doe is a qualified teacher; they already know because they know the membership.

(3) We know you. A third advantage to hiring from within is that the institutional loyalty of such staff members is already known. Because they are already committed to this church, they are more likely to see their ministry as a labor of love rather than just a set of duties to perform, and almost certainly not as a stepping stone to a better job

somewhere else. Not only will the loyalty to the church have been established for current members seeking employment, their loyalty to the other members of the staff will have been established as well; they already have a track record of cooperation, participation, and interaction with other staff members. Also, because persons already inside the congregation are known to the leadership, it is easier to assess their character. I do not have to verbalize my four questions directly; I have seen the answers over the course of time.

Although these three advantages are weighty, there are at least two negative aspects to hiring from within.

(1) What happens if it just doesn't work out? First, recruiting someone who is already fully committed to the church through long-term, active participation can be a double-edged sword. How do you release an employee who is also a much beloved member if that person just does not work out? To do so, even if it is justified, may create much bloodshed. For this very reason, in former times, and in some places still today, many churches had expressed policies prohibiting the hiring of church members. But such a policy is too restrictive; there are important advantages to be gleaned, as enumerated above. What is essential is that the selection be made carefully such that no "duds" are hired. The dismissal of any beloved employee, whether originally from inside the church or outside, is a painful and difficult undertaking. Practically speaking, after staff members have been on duty for three years or longer, they have effectively become insiders.

As a general rule, I would rather hire secretarial and cus-todial help from outside the congregation, but program staff from within. The reason for this has to do with the nature of the work each does. As Ken Callahan points out in his book *The Twelve Keys to an Effective Church*,[1] the church has two sorts of work. One of these can be the source of satisfaction, whereas the other can be the source of dissatisfaction. More to the point, the secretarial and custodial functions are connected only to a potential source of dissatisfaction. That is, if both of these are well attended to, the congregation will not then be "happy." Virtually nothing that the support staff ever does can cause the membership to be satisfied. On the other hand, support staff can cause the congregation to grumble if their work is inadequate. "Satisfiers" are generally ministry items. This is not to say that no one appreciates secretaries and custodians, but in general, too few people really do. For these reasons, I believe that it might be discouraging for church members who share their congregation's values and who see themselves as being in ministry amongst their own people to discover that their church family appears to be unappreciative. Program and ministry staffers, however, can bring "satisfaction" to the congregation simply by doing their jobs well, and are therefore not likely to experience their church as ungrateful. In this case, church members who take on ministry and program roles will enjoy positive feedback from the people who mean the most to them—a good deal for staff and congregation alike.

(2) We may not get any boost with an insider. The second disadvantage of hiring from within is the likelihood that the church will miss the phenomenon I call the "oomph factor." What I am referring to is the sense of renewal and added spark that comes when a new leader hits town. The "oomph factor" can be seen in the popularity polls and "approval ratings" that jump up, often dramatically, when a newly elected official takes the oath of office. Without having done anything yet, the new person is seen as inspiring, and the people experience a sense of hope welling up from within their own hearts. For this reason we mark the first one hundred days of a new president's administration; likewise, newly installed pastors go

through a "honeymoon" period where the members are willing to give their new leader a chance and are willing to listen with an open mind to almost any new suggestion, including ones that would have been totally unacceptable had the predecessor made them two months earlier. If, however, the new staff member is "merely a regular person whom we already know to be just like us," then there is little "oomph" that occurs. This is doubly the case if the church member has already been functioning in the position for which they are now hired. However, two circumstances are to be considered in this regard. First, if the would-be staff member is functioning well in the position, perhaps a momentary "oomph" is unnecessary. After all, it is the long-term that counts, and a truly effective staff member is to be cherished. Second, if the position is altogether new, that position itself will generate an excitement all its own; thus, the thrill of the "new" is still experienced. If, however, a program is stuck on "high center," I would be more inclined to look outside the congregation for new leadership in order to recharge its energy system.

Making a Team out of the Players

As stated in the first part of this chapter, it is essential, especially as we are entering a new millennium, to work in teams. Many excellent resources on team ministry have been written, and I will not attempt to rehash those here. For my purposes, I want only to acknowledge the power of such a concept. When staff members understand in the depths of their being that we are indeed the Body of Christ, as the Scriptures have asserted for two thousand years, it liberates individual leaders who have always thought that they had to "go it alone" or "be the star." It often also liberates hidden talents and unsuspected abilities. For example, some of the finest, most forward-looking suggestions for enhancing our facilities have come from our minister of music. Likewise, our children's minister has helped plan some very inspiring worship experiences. All of this has been done without the old-style turf protection of the past. Recently our youth minister took on an intern, a very bright and creative young man. Our director, an experienced veteran of ten years, has found himself asking, "What if this guy is a better Sunday school teacher and a better youth counselor than I am? What then?" His answer finally was, "Praise God! We're not in competition. In fact, one of the key ingredients to my job is to assist folks to discover their spiritual gifts and employ them for Christ. There is plenty of work for us all."

The crucial issue here is for godly, committed servants of Christ to truly practice what every minister of the gospel preaches every week—that we are indeed fully interdependent. The biggest impediment we face is the pervasive cultural value of excessive individualism. Ironically, American Protestantism has long been held captive to such a misunderstanding of reality, even though the Scriptures are quite clear that we are connected, whether we acknowledge it or not. Jesus prayed to the Father, "that [the church] may be one, as we are one" in his high priestly prayer in the Garden of Gethsemane shortly before his crucifixion (John 17:22). The church should never have lost sight of this truth. Fortunately, with the emergence of the "Baby Buster" generation, a corrective to our excessive individualism seems to be forthcoming. To maximize its effectiveness, a church staff must become a team as a whole and a series of subteams with fellow staff members and laity. The trick is to contribute to the work for which another is responsible without challenging that person's authority. Again, the attitude of the participants is the essential ingredient, born of a lived theology of mutuality within the Body of Christ.

CHAPTER 10

SECOND THOUGHTS

I believe that we have done several things well—some by design and some by accident—and God has indeed blessed our efforts. Lyle Schaller "twisted my arm" to write this book to tell about our church and its turnaround. However, as I confessed to him, if I tell only those things that are positive, I will fail to tell the whole truth and thereby give a false impression of invulnerability and unmitigated success. On most days I see failings as well as successes, and feel commensurate discouragement alongside a healthy pride. The essential thing is not whether or not we have failed; we have—repeatedly. The question is, "What next? How can we get back up and go again? Indeed, how can we even use our failures for the glory of God?"

Among my failings are both sins of commission and sins of omission. In the latter category, the list is lengthy. For example, I have been too slow to push our evangelistic efforts forward. I know that we could have gotten many more "names on the dotted line" had I been more aggressive; however, I deferred. My excuses centered around our lack of assimilation and my own time constraints, but these are just excuses. Surely we could have done better. Surely I could have done better. In a like manner, any number of other ministries could have been created had I done things differently. What about a viable singles program? Why haven't we started that Saturday night service? And the list goes on. Although one can always mourn opportunities lost, it is in the things that we actually do, the missteps that we take, that we can discover how to handle failure best.

The Battle of the Budget: The Setup

Perhaps the most obvious example of a failure that I perpetrated occurred in December of 1996. We were preparing for our annual charge conference, the "big meeting of the year" when officers are elected, priorities are adopted, and budgets are set. Recent days had been filled with triumph, or so it seemed to me. During the first two years of my tenure, our church had met or exceeded its budget. This was a great turnaround, for in ten of the eleven prior years, our congregation had failed to meet its budget and instead had been forced to dip into its reserves just to stay afloat. The reserves were almost entirely depleted over that period of time. Needless to say, the congregation was delighted to have met its budget in 1994 and again in 1995. Likewise, in the fall of 1996 as I looked at the overall trends, it seemed apparent that we sat poised to duplicate the feat yet again.

As I had been encouraged to do by our finance people during the previous two budgeting cycles, I worked with the various entities within the church on their requests for 1997 funding, trying to plan modest, but real, increases to keep our church growing. We made the painful choices that are always required for a church budget, balancing the various interests within the congregation for staff raises, program expansion, and facilities needs. The proposed 1997 budget totaled a workable 4 percent overall increase. In light of the just completed capital stewardship program, this seemed a prudent amount. The final steps in the process were to send the budget to the Finance Committee, who would then forward it to the charge conference for official approval.

A kink in the system emerged, however, at the Finance

Committee. Let me note that I do not attend every meeting of every committee in the church. In fact, to do so is impossible because we stack the assembly of most of our administrative bodies on the same evening each month. As usual, on the particular night in question, several committees were in session. Believing that the finance committee's vote was pro forma, I elected to attend the meeting of another group who needed me more. It was several days later when I learned that the finance committee had carried on a rather heated debate about the 1997 proposal. Many wanted to approve the budget as presented, but some were very much afraid that we would not be able to attain it. Further, they believed that the success of the capital funds campaign almost ensured that we would experience a dip in budgetary receipts, not only in 1997 but also at the end of 1996. They feared that we would fail to meet our 1996 target, that we would revert to the longer-standing pattern of earlier years, further diminishing our reserves. Their logic, I concluded, went something like this, "Yes, we told people during the capital funds campaign that their building fund pledges must be over and above their regular church giving, that to take from the church budget in order to finance a building program would collapse the whole system. Yes, we said this repeatedly, but the average member is either (a) too stupid to hear and understand this line of reasoning or (b) willingly rebellious against it. Either way, many members have probably rechanneled their budget giving into the building fund, and we will not be able to attain our budget projections." Through the tone of my description, perhaps the reader will already have picked up on my assessment of the finance committee's rationale. Simply stated, I believed they were grossly mistaken.

However much we finally tally each year, one thing is certain: we will raise at least 20 percent of our total receipts during December, and 1996 was lining up as no exception.

That is, when December arrived we would be just over 20 percent away from full funding. Since the 1996 budget was the largest in our history, the total of dollars outstanding appeared to certain finance folks as an impossible amount to be raised in such a short time. Further, some committee members feared that congregational members would immediately turn some of their resources to the capital campaign, and that they would keep up the practice in 1997. From my perspective, if only the committee had taken an unbiased and rational look at long-term trends, they would know that we were in line to finish the year in the black.

The Battle of the Budget: A Fateful Decision

The decision by the finance committee was to take no action whatsoever until they saw with their own eyes what totals would finally be raised in 1996. They believed that the responsible course was to postpone adopting a new budget until 1996 was complete and all receipts were counted. If we achieved our budget for 1996, they reasoned, we could then adopt the 1997 proposal with its 4 percent increase.

This decision did not sit well with me for two reasons. First, their thinking seemed to fit the classic "all-or-nothing" error: "Either we achieve 100 percent of our 1996 budget, or we cannot possibly raise the 1997 version by even one cent." What if we got within 3 percent of the 1996 budget, paid all of our bills, and were operating just fine? Could we then raise the 1997 figure by, say, 3 percent rather than the proposed 4 percent? What if our shortfall turns out to be just 1 percent, or what if we miss our total by only $200? There was no flexibility in the formula, at least as it was reported to me. The second reason I disliked the finance committee's strategy was far more serious, for as I saw it, the real issue we faced was not finances, but faith.

God had blessed us in so many ways. We were "on a roll," financially and spiritually. We had just completed the largest and the most successful capital funds campaign in our history, one whose actual results exceeded the wildest dreams of anyone in the church. Attendance was up markedly. Enthusiasm was high in every quarter. Building remodeling was going on all around us. Clearly, God was blessing our church. "So," I reasoned, "are we now to believe that God will somehow shut off the faucet of blessing? Will the Lord who has 'blessed the socks off of us' suddenly shout, 'Enough!'?" It was clear to me that the finance committee was motivated by fear; moreover, they were "living in the past," remembering the difficult years that had now been replaced by God's bounty. The primary issue, then, was spiritual, "Will we live by fear, based on past hurts; or will we live by faith, based upon God's very real, present-tense blessing?"

The Battle of the Budget: Counterattacks One and Two

I spoke to the chairperson of the finance committee, telling her that I believed that the course of action laid out by the committee was an act of *unfaith*. To pursue it would put us in jeopardy that God might indeed cut off the blessing—not because our folks had misdirected their pledges from the general fund to the building fund, but because we were choosing to live by sight and not by faith. Real faith is not irrational, I agreed, but this decision was. The chairperson was mildly sympathetic, but said that there was nothing she could do. By this time, I was genuinely afraid that our church was in danger of committing spiritual suicide. During the two weeks that preceded the charge conference, I prayed more than I had at any other time in the previous five years.

All of this was, in a very real sense, incredibly ironic. In previous years I had advocated that our annual conference change its practice so that local church charge conferences would be held annually after the turn of the new year. My reasoning was practical: it seems silly to me for the church to compile statistics for a charge conference meeting in the fall that will shortly be replaced by end-of-the-year figures, the only ones that are permanently retained. Why not wait until the books are finally closed to compile a single, meaningful report? The issue at stake at Lake Highlands in the fall of 1996, however, was not institutional-process duplication (which I wanted to eliminate), but instead struck at the heart of our relationship with almighty God. Would we live by faith, or not?

A second avenue of appeal, it seemed to me, lay in the staff-parish committee. In our system, the staff-parish committee has both the right and the responsibility to recommend salaries to the charge conference, and can "buck" the finance committee if there is a difference of opinion. That is, the finance committee exercises advisory, rather than veto, power over some portions of the budget. I believed that the staff-parish committee, who had worked rather diligently to hold their recommendation to 4 percent, might not simply acquiesce to the misguided overcautiousness of the finance committee. I spoke with the chair and with one other member of this nine-person body, telling them of my alarm. They both listened with interest; one stated that I might be right, whereas the other flatly told me that she wished she had as much faith as I, but that she too was afraid that we would not meet our budget target.

Just days before the big annual meeting, I learned that the staff-parish committee had conducted a telephone poll (rather than hold a face-to-face meeting) and had elected not to fight the recommendation of the finance committee. It was almost inconceivable to me that no one would stand up and say, "Hold on, folks. Might we be making a mistake here?" I was angry, hurt, and afraid. My wife and I wondered if it might be time to request a move; I did not want to preside over a church "going down the tubes" because God's blessing had been rejected in favor of fear. I felt that my leadership had also been rejected.

The Battle of the Budget: Dropping the Bomb

I could find no sense of peace as the day of the charge conference approached. I did know, however, that I could not remain silent. I finally discovered a measure of ease through prayer, becoming convinced that, although we were indeed exercising unfaith, God would not withdraw heaven's blessing this time. However, I knew that unfaith cannot continue forever.

One of the standard reports at the charge conference is the pastor's "State of the Church" address, and I decided that I would use that vehicle to sound the alarm. Just before going into the meeting, I warned my district superintendent, who was presiding, that I would issue a strong rebuke to the assembled leaders. He was a little taken aback, but did not attempt to dissuade me (which would have been futile in any case). I had scheduled myself to be last on the agenda. With great anxiety, I read a carefully worded statement, outlining my assessment of the issue. I began by reminding the assembled leaders of the great strides we had made in 1996 and celebrating with them the obvious presence of God in our midst. But then, I let down the hammer:

A few minutes ago, I believe we exercised "unfaith" toward God. Faith, if it is worthy of the name, requires that we seek to discern God's will, listening for his call and seeking his leadership in our lives. Real faith requires that we step out in obedience to God, going where we sense God is leading us. Over the last two years, God has indeed blessed our common life together. Our church has grown in every measurable way until today we stand at all-time highs in attendance, membership, and giving. We have met our budget for the last two years, a feat accomplished only once in the previous ten years. Likewise, we have just concluded the most successful capital funds campaign in our history, receiving commitments for $1.8 million over and above our current giving.

All of this is to be expected if we are faithful to God. However, despite God's abundant blessing in our lives, we have just told God with our vote that we believe he either cannot or will not continue blessing us, that we believe that we cannot raise as much money as we thought previously and that we had better take shelter.

I believe that this represents a break in our faith. Rather than depending on the God who has delivered so abundantly in the last two years, we suddenly have cold feet and think that we are relying only on ourselves. Further, we don't believe that we can do it either, so we voted to keep a flatline budget for 1997.... What does this mean? I believe that we are in the untenable position of trying to be a church of God while relying on our own strength. We can certainly choose to go down that path. But if we do, at some point God, who has a will for us that we are rejecting because we can't believe that he can or will bless us that much—this God will ultimately, sadly shake his head and say to us, "Okay, not my will, but thine be done." If he does this, we will be right about ourselves; we will not be able to raise the 1996 budget. But it will not just be in 1996; it will also be in 1997 and 1998 and 1999. If we disbelieve God, we place ourselves in mortal jeopardy.

I then reassured my hearers that I was convinced that God would give us another "chance," that we would indeed reach our budget in 1996. I observed that I had never before made a speech like this, and that it was most difficult for me to do so, yet I felt compelled to. "I cannot hold my tongue and still call myself a minister of Christ." Many in the room did not know of the finance committee's decision until I read the report, for little fanfare had been made of it outside of the two bodies previously named. I concluded by telling the charge conference that I did not want them to amend the actions they had heretofore taken, but to think upon the message that I had delivered. I was unwilling to manipulate the meeting's outcome through strong-arm tactics.

The Battle of the Budget: Rocked by the Aftershock

At the close of the charge conference, I felt miserable. I normally seek to avoid confrontation whenever possible, and this was particularly painful to me. Surprisingly, several council members congratulated me for exercising "strong leadership." Some said it was "long overdue." Nevertheless, I still felt badly.

Two days later, I received a very painful note from some trusted friends, alerting me that they were withdrawing their pledge from the church because they were not sure they could continue in a church with a "leader who believes he is the only one who can hear from God." That stung. I called immediately, requesting a time to visit in their home. Upon arrival, we jumped deeply into a most instructive conversation. One member of the couple sits on the staff-parish committee. This person was particularly hurt that I had not aired my concerns to their committee. If God had spoken to me, and if they were also open to God, surely we could have reached a meeting of minds. But there had been no meeting. Although the chair did not call one, as the pastor I could have done so, rather than "lying in wait" to lash out at them in a public meeting. And why had I not talked to the finance committee if I was so disconcerted? Why wait until the charge conference?

They were right, and, oh, how it hurt to hear it! Why hadn't I called a special meeting of both finance and staff-parish committees? Yes, time was limited, but by my own declaration, nothing we were doing was of any more urgency. Instead, I had "ambushed" these people, whom I professed to love, in front of their fellow church members, publicly shaming some of the most faithful members of our church.

This was a miscalculation of monumental proportions. Mind you, I was still convinced that my point was absolutely on target. But my methods were hideously wrong. My zeal had overshadowed my judgment, and the only question remaining in my mind was, "Have I stumbled so badly that I have poisoned my leadership here?"

The Battle of the Budget: Making a Christian Peace

However my question would be answered, I knew that I owed an apology to those persons whom I had offended. A principle that I have always followed is that confession should be made to as broad a group as the sin is known. Since my broadside against the finance and staff-parish committees had been public, I decided on a twofold course of action. First, I sent a letter of apology to all members of the charge conference and all other guests who had signed in that night. Second, I issued a brief statement of apology on Sunday morning directly from the pulpit. Here is the statement as I read it.

Whenever human beings share life together, problems are bound to arise, sometimes grievous, hurtful problems. This is true even when those people love and respect each other, and even when they act from good motives. That is, caring people, operating out of good motives, sometimes injure the ones they most mean to help.

Such an incident occurred this past week—at the charge conference. It was in that meeting that one of our own stood before the body assembled there and, out of what he thought was a pure motivation, castigated the elected leaders of the church. What he intended as the sounding of an alarm to call Lake Highlands to faithful discipleship came across to many in the room as a self-righteous, wholesale condemnation of the entire church. Many of our elected leaders were shocked and deeply wounded by this rebuke, and a rift has occurred in the Body of Christ.

I am the one who has perpetrated this offense, and I stand before you today to offer my apology for grieving the Body. Let me be clear: I stand by what I asserted about the danger of not exercising faith in all our actions. We must be more than a human institution as the Church of Jesus Christ. But that is a subject for another day. Right now we must deal with the rift that I have caused with my speech. I was wrong—a thousand times wrong—to make a public pronouncement at the charge conference before first airing the issues with the individual commit-tees. Herein lies my sin, in not calling the respective com-mittees together to discuss the issues that so possessed my mind and heart.

You may wonder why I am offering a public apology today. The Scriptures teach us that one's confession of sin should be as public as one's commission of sin. Since the charge conference is a public forum, open to the whole church, I feel obliged to declare my repentance publicly as well. I ask for your pardon for the hurt that I have inflicted upon us all.

I believe that mine was an error of the head and not of the heart. I care about this congregation deeply, so much so that I felt willing to risk misunderstanding and dis-agreement by making my declaration at the charge con-ference. It's only a true friend who will tell you the things he knows you won't like. That was the spirit in which I meant my speech. It was not received that way, for which I am profoundly sorry.

My prayer is that we can heal from this hurtful incident and even grow from it. But I also know that many feel that I have violated their trust. And it takes time, as well as God's grace, to overcome such a violation.

Some day I hope that we can discuss the issue that I meant to speak with you about, but which I failed to communicate. For now, please pray for me and for healing within the Body of Christ.

The Battle of the Budget: The Aftermath of War

It appears that my apology was accepted by those who were most offended. My friends, who were bold enough to write my initial wake-up letter, are still friends and have reinstated their pledge. As far as I can tell, no one left the church over the affair. It was a most difficult incident, and perhaps a watershed event in some ways. Had I not made the apology, I believe that I would have lost credibility with a number of key leaders. Indeed, the laity of my church might well have become afraid to make any decisions for fear that their pastor would publicly ridicule them if he disliked those decisions. To fail to apologize would have been disastrous.

On the positive side, I believe that through the incident I became a bit more "human" to many of the members of my congregation. They got to see me in my failure. Although everyone knows that we are all sinners, we don't always see our leader's troubles. All too often we place such folks on pedestals. I hope that they also got an object lesson in how to deal with one's sin. It is essential that we not cover up our sins. We must not blame them on "those people who made me do it." Rather, we are to take responsibility for our own actions, regardless of the motives that drove us or the justice of our position. In the final analysis, these are learnings that are crucial for all human beings. Although I was not pleased to have made such public spectacle of myself, I trust that God used even my folly for his glory. This is the mystery and the majesty of the great God whom we serve. Sometimes, as the apostle Paul noted, God's strength is seen most clearly in our weakness, and the all-sufficiency of God's grace shines forth when we reach the end of ourselves.[1]

CHAPTER 11

WHAT NEXT?

The reason that Lake Highlands United Methodist Church has a story to tell is that God has granted us a vision. We have tried to live faithfully by that vision. We understand ourselves to be in the disciple-making business; our main job is to relate folks to God in Christ and help them mature in their discipleship. Our methods for fulfilling this mission have diversified in recent years. We have launched a contemporary worship experience; we are building a new building; we are planting new congregations in apartment communities. But we are not finished visioning because God is not finished with us yet. Even if we do perfectly and abundantly those things that we have set our hearts and hands to, our ministry will be incomplete. God's Spirit, as Jesus told us, is like the wind; the Spirit goes in directions we are not prepared for. Or, as a friend of mine is fond of saying, "God is predictably unpredictable." I believe that the unpredictable God is signaling a new and challenging turn onto a path that we have never traveled before. Many unreached peoples still drive past our facilities every day, and we cannot rest on yesterday's accomplishments or today's efforts as long as that is the case.

Three Innovations to Come

Yes, in the next few years we will attempt a number of innovations. Three are on the immediate drawing board.

First, we are launching our own homepage on the World Wide Web, as are numerous congregations of various stripes. We believe that this will enable us to reach computer-literate audiences in certain ways; and as the Web becomes more widely used, our homepage will eventually improve communication with our whole church membership. Second, we hope to become a "teaching church," training other congregations to develop their own off-campus ministries. We believe that other churches can catch our vision and our passion for this work by spending two to three days with us. Right now we have a story to tell; soon we will have a whole ministry to show. Third, we anticipate launching a full-blown contemporary service on Saturday evenings within the next two years. Our Roman Catholic brethren have proved to us that there is a high demand for alternative worship times, and Saturday evening appears to be ideal. Our target audience will be younger persons who do not want to get up early on Sunday but who may be willing to give Jesus a try before going out on the town on Saturday night.

Unapproved Possibilities

If we continue to grow, the time will come when Lake Highlands Church will need to develop a second campus. It is difficult to grow when the parking lot is filled beyond capacity, as ours is. (People park on the grass, in the alley, and on the pavement directly behind another vehicle, thus blocking them in.) And if the voucher system for school choice ever passes, we will probably open a Christian day school. We might even sell our current complex to such a school and relocate entirely. But such matters are still in the conjecture stage.

God Communicates a New Vision

Important as the preceding visions are, they pale in comparison to the new direction in which God is leading us during the next few years. God has woven several strands together in my mind in recent months to form a tapestry of need that has caught my attention. First, a piece of biography: I have three daughters. Throughout their growing-up years, I have heard pleas for permission to "stay out later for this particular dance, Dad. You don't understand; it's Homecoming; everyone is doing it." Of course, I always wonder whether my child is an accurate reporter. Is it true that *everyone* is doing this, or just the kids she is hanging out with? Or perhaps even more plausible, are her friends telling their parents that *everyone,* including the Methodist preacher's daughter, is staying out late as *their* justification? Either way, it dawned on me that whatever the community standards are, I was not participating in their establishment, at least not consciously. Who sets those standards, I wondered?

A second strand tickles my imagination every Lord's Day when we participate in holy baptism, particularly when a baby is brought before the altar of God. During the service the parents promise to raise this precious infant in the way of Christ. They are asked to bring the child to church faithfully, as well as teach the baby themselves, both by precept and by example. They must answer yes to each question of this nature before water is extended.

After such children are baptized, I, as the minister, proudly and lovingly parade them before the congregation. In the presence of all there assembled, I speak directly to the babies, who usually look amused as I speak. I tell these new initiates into the family of God that the folks in front of them are in fact their spiritual family, that everyone seated in these pews will love them and will answer all their questions. "It's easy to answer their questions now," I sometimes prompt the congregation, "because they can't yet speak. But you had better get to studying; this baby is growing rapidly." Then comes the mysterious part. I ask the congregation to stand and turn to page 44 of the Hymnal, where I read this charge:

Members of the household of faith, I commend to your love and care *this child*, whom we this day recognize as *a member* of the family of God. Will you endeavor so to live that *this child* may grow in the knowledge and love of God, through our Savior Jesus Christ?

The congregation then reads this response:

With God's help we will so order our lives after the example of Christ, that *this child*, surrounded by steadfast love, may be established in the faith, and confirmed and strengthened in the way that leads to life eternal.

Each time we enact this ritual, I wonder to myself how many of the people here are really pledging themselves to help raise this child in the way of faith. What specifically and tangibly will they do to help these parents? If they see this little boy eight years from now chucking rocks at a streetlight, will they stop their car and intervene? After all, they have promised. Or, more likely, will they simply drive on, all the while complaining about the "Jones boy becoming a delinquent"? Those baptismal vows make me uncomfortable.

A third strand begging for attention came in a conversation with Lyle Schaller. "How do you grow a megachurch?" I asked. His response was startling, "It's easy!" Easy? I like easy. So how? He continued, "If you want to grow a megachurch, all you have to do is go out to that nearby freeway and rent three or four billboards. On them, just write a simple question: 'Need help with your family? Call [*fill in the blank with your church's phone number*].' But now comes the hard part. When they call, you have to be able to deliver." When he said this, I knew instantly that he was right. People struggle most with their most intimate relationships: "How can I bring life to my listless marriage? How can I reach my teenage son? Why can't my daughter and I talk without screaming? If I'm such a success at work, why doesn't anyone at home even like me? I'm depressed and drowning, does anybody care?"

The fourth strand of the tapestry that led to our next vision came when we were planning programs for the new year. I felt a great deal of pride when our highly competent director of children's ministries outlined the plan for another year's excellent children's programming. Likewise, the youth department is strong, complete with a one-hundred-voice youth choir, great youth mission trips, a clown ministry, the ACT musical, and lots more. We also enjoy some strong adult programming, including an exceptional adult Sunday school, quality Bible studies, and meaningful covenant discipleship groups. Finally, we have a top flight older adult ministry that has recently featured programs with a world-renowned artist and with the Dallas chief of police, as well as some excellent trips across the country. "Yes, we have something for the whole family," I thought smugly. But suddenly it dawned upon me: "We have something for the whole family, but we don't actually do anything for the family as a whole!" True, we have a family life commission, but, like its counterpart in so many other congregations, that role has generally been relegated to organizing a couple of covered-dish dinners and a family picnic each year. When it comes to the hopes and hurts of real families, we have little to offer.

The Controlling Image

In Luke 2 we find the account of Jesus and his family traveling up to Jerusalem to celebrate the Passover feast. In that era it was normative for every good Jewish family to travel to Jerusalem at Passover. Jesus was then twelve years old. When we pick up the scene in verse 44, the feast is over. Meanwhile, Mary and Joseph have traveled a whole day's journey back toward Nazareth when, to their horror, they discover that Jesus was not among the caravan's many pilgrims. They, of course, return to Jerusalem immediately, and only after three days of searching do they finally find Jesus again. Reading the story through twentieth-century eyes, we wonder how in the world good parents could travel a whole day and night before detecting that their son was missing. Is this not tantamount to neglect? The answer, of course, is no, this is not neglect. We do not have a case of bad parents, but bad social sensitivity by us.

When Mary and Joseph took the young Jesus up to Jerusalem, they did not go alone. Rather, they were but one family among a whole community of families, all on a spiritual journey together. On the way it was only natural that Jesus and Benjamin and James and Philip would spend the morning walking with, say, Abraham's family because Abraham was crippled and needed help carrying his supplies. For lunch, the boys would stop by Philip's tent, since Philip's mother was the best cook and always made date cookies. And at night everyone wanted to stay at Benjamin's tent because his dad was the best storyteller in the community. Meanwhile the mothers told their sons not to burden any particular family too much. But worry? Never. They were all safe together because they *were all together.* Each member of the community had something to offer; all were appreciated for their contributions and all found help from their fellow pilgrims along the way. They were a *family of families on a spiritual journey.*

I believe that the church ought also to be a family of families on a spiritual journey. That in fact has become the controlling image that is guiding our new vision. Yes, we ought to be a family of families, but we are not. Rather, we are a collection of individuals. True, many of us come to church with other members of our family, yet in truth we are still all alone. At best, most churches contain individual pilgrims on individual spiritual journeys—not in community, though in the same church, and certainly not as a family. Our intention is to transform the basis upon which we build our church.

Moving from Dreaming to Planning

What I have described thus far is only a vision; to become a reality requires the development of a plan, one that has the power to transform the entire system at Lake Highlands. If we are to be successful at implementing this vision, we must change a large number of the ministries of our church, and even more fundamentally, we must reconceptualize church itself. To do so will be painful. If we started from a blank slate—that is, if we were to launch a new congregation— it would be much easier than to make this radical shift. It is, after all, easier to born a baby than to raise the dead. But the call of God is to bring a transformation here among these people, and thankfully our God has proved rather good at resurrections.

To bring the vision into reality, I began to disseminate the basic concept more than a year in advance in a one-on-one fashion, building support with a few key persons who I believed might have a natural affinity for it. The next step was to share the dream at a planning/visioning retreat. The body gathered that day had the authority to move us toward its implementation. Indeed, following my presentation several wanted to adopt the "Family Church" as our "program emphasis for the year" on the spot. The concept resonated with our folks, which was an important authentication of its validity. However, having primed the chairperson of the council in advance, we resisted this option, knowing that to declare ourselves a "Family Church" without the hard planning necessary to bring it off would be self-defeating. We did, however, encourage every committee, commission, board, agency, and group in the church to consider ways in which they might build families into their own programming over the course of the next year. Likewise, we resisted lodging the planning function in a standing committee, where its fate would have been uncertain at best. Committees already have full plates and generally are not very creative. To merely add another item onto a standing committee's agenda would not likely produce the big results we sought.

We asked for and received the authority to appoint (not elect) a task force whose responsibility would be to develop a "turn-key plan." By allowing the chair and myself to appoint the task force members, we enjoyed three advantages. (1) We could be free of the usual "quota system" ("We need an elderly woman from the Mary-Martha Class to balance the young men on the committee."). (2) We could be flexible enough to add additional members as creative people were uncovered because we did not have a designated number of slots. (3) We were able to use some highly competent newer members who, because they were newer, would not otherwise be elected.

Staff Involvement in the Planning Process

The resolution that I proposed stated that no member of the church staff would be a member of the task force, although all staff members would be available to the task force for counsel and leg work. This meant that the staff would neither control nor subvert the process. Although our staff has been very supportive of the "Family Church" concept, I knew that it was possible that they might potentially undermine the process if they saw its direction becoming a threat to them in any of three key areas: (1) their turf—"You're taking away my favorite program that we do every summer"; (2) their job security—"With the addition of a new Family Ministries Director, my own job might be reduced to part-time"; or (3) their work load—"If

we do this, I'll be up at that church four nights a week."
Persons who have a vested interest to protect tend not to
provide great creativity.

The Six Pillars of a Family Church

The assignment was simple in one sense: envision what
our church would be like if this vision were fully opera-
tional, and from that full-blown program work back-
wards, detailing all the steps that will be necessary to
move us from here to there. What will it take to transform
us from a collection of individuals, each working on our
own private versions of Christian growth, to a family of
families together on a spiritual journey? To help understand this vision, I proposed six pillars of a true "Family
Church."

(1) *Support Groups.* Any number of family problems
attack the nucleus of the family structure, from divorce to
serious illness. Often such difficulties can leave a family
reeling, disoriented, and losing perspective on the rest of
life. Often the tenderest, best answers to such difficulties
can be found in fellowship with others who likewise are
encountering the same calamities or have recently been
through them. Just as various pilgrims on the road to
Jerusalem with Mary and Joseph could assist each other, so
can persons struggling with a similar crisis help us as we
travel down the same road. A modern equivalent is the
support group. Any number of crisis-specific groups can be
envisioned: Families Anonymous, networking parents who
have teenagers involved in drugs; divorce-recovery
groups; grief-recovery groups; Attention Deficit Disorder
support groups. The list goes on. In recent years the church
across America has done well in instituting support
groups. In our own setting, we already sponsor a Families
Anonymous group; an ACAP/P group for adults with

aging parents; and ACES, which assists single parents seeking child support. What we lack is an overall plan to touch the needs of people in crisis.

(2) Family Forums. "Family Forums" (we are looking for a better term) stand at the heart of the "Family Church" concept. Their central purposes are fourfold: (a) to assist our members in socializing with similarly situated families; (b) to help them interact in meaningful ways; (c) to provide a mechanism in which to "test reality" about what is actually going on within the Lake Highlands area that affects our families; and (d) to establish and support our own "community standards" and "community values." Professionals, as well as other resource persons, will be called upon periodically to provide helpful information about the wider neighborhood. Occasional outside speakers from the police department and the school district, psychologists, and child development experts will add their input on current realities facing us. For example, we may host a gang-awareness forum to which we invite police and school counselors, plus other experts in the field to discuss this particular problem with families of older elementary and junior high school youth.

The real focus of the "Family Forum," however, is on providing a vehicle for community-building in which families discuss issues and counsel each other. Included might be premarital workshops; pre-parental workshops; new mother's training and discussion groups; parents' discussion groups to assist each other in dealing with classic issues confronted by families with preschool and elementary school children (to spank or not to spank? what activity is age-appropriate for a six-year-old's birthday party? and lots more); and opportunities for teens and their parents to discuss the issues they face (setting a "community standard" for curfews for fifteen-year-olds, and so on).

Always our underlying goal is to create a true community in which everyone has a part in helping the whole.

(3) *Family Counseling.* Sometimes family problems move beyond the stage in which family forums or even support groups are adequate. In such cases, professional help is needed. We live in an area in which there are numerous counseling services available, and every week or two I am asked either to do counseling or for the name of a counselor who can help a hurting person or family. Over the years I have developed lists of counselors whom I consider competent and who are not likely to direct my members into some course of action contrary to Christian values.

What is missing from many therapeutic settings, however, is the ability to meet individuals in the larger environment in which they live. In simple terms, it does little good to "fix" clients but then return them to the same unhealthy environment that fostered their problems in the first place. For that reason, family systems theory has been developed and practiced with excellent results in recent years. But why not take that one step further? Why not provide professional help to individuals, and especially to families, in the context of a larger community environment? If the therapist were also part of the community, she would have all the skills of her trade, but with the added resource of a coordinated family-friendly church community to add to the treatment. Thus, the therapist, as part of her treatment regimen, may suggest that the client family join a "Family Forum" or become active in family-oriented recreational activities. Knowing that such options are available and which ones of them offer the greatest potential benefit could add a whole new dimension to the therapeutic process. Likewise, when clients have completed counseling, they may have established new, healthy community bonds that are so necessary for continued emotional stability and personal growth. And even if the therapist does not choose the option of plugging clients into some of the other family ministries, it is still both worthwhile and significant that hurting human beings find assistance (therapy) within the Christian community. After all, psychology itself arose within the church, the art being known as "the cure of souls." How appropriate that the church assist in curing souls today.

In practical terms, I believe that we will eventually have a licensed family therapist on staff. Of course, we would build into the system all of the safeguards for privacy and protection of clients that is appropriate. We will certainly not attempt to tell the therapist how to do her job. But we will have available an entire community of healing, a feature missing from even the most progressive of treatment centers.

(4) Special-Needs Assistance. Many families encounter special needs that cannot be neatly "fixed" simply by joining a group or even through counseling. For example, families in which there is no father present face issues that two-parent homes do not encounter. The children in such families do not typically see healthy interaction between husband and wife and between father and child on any regular basis. Where will they experience healthy role models? As the product of a broken home myself, I know firsthand what an issue this can be. As a child I looked for an answer to the very real question, "What is *normal?*" I certainly did not know. For role models, then, I ultimately turned to Ward and June Cleaver, the parents on television's *Leave It to Beaver.* Although not terribly realistic as role models, Ward and June were at least wholesome and were not opposed to traditional Christian values. Is it not somewhat frightening to imagine that children today may be looking to television's Roseanne Barr to answer the same question? The single parent in such a household also

has many other challenges to face: How do I get my shopping done? What can I do with my kids while I go out? Can I ever have any time alone at home? The issue we want to address is how our community can meet these and other special needs.

One answer may be to provide surrogate extended families. In such a model, children from single-parent homes may be paired with intact two-parent families (let's call them "Kissin' Cousin Families") with similarly aged children. The children from the single-parent home may spend every other Friday night through Saturday afternoon with the "Cousin Family." This gives the children the opportunity to experience a working two-parent family, while at the same time providing the single parent with a much needed "breather." Other special needs may be found among the elderly who are without nuclear family nearby. Single individuals have special needs as well. Counting singles as a special-needs family is, I believe, a more healthy model than the typical "meat-market" approach to singles ministry. Special-needs ministries is a fertile and burgeoning field, desperately in need of tending.

(5) *Connecting the Generations.* We need to provide mechanisms that foster interaction between the generations. Certainly the family forums will frequently connect the generations, but this is too limited because it often will exclude singles, older persons, and families without dependent children. Perhaps the best meeting places for the generations are in fields of service. Off-Campus Ministries already provides this sort of opportunity, and indeed, we will use this angle as a mechanism for attracting new volunteer families.

For example, several of our families with elementary-school-age children regularly work with children in one of our apartment locations. The children, no less than the

parents, look forward to sharing their lives with the apartment communities, and actually serve as a catalyst to the
parents to continue with that ministry through difficult
days.

I believe that we have one-upped the old adage, "The
family that prays together, stays together." As family
members help each other to give of themselves, they will
view each other in a different light. Certainly they will
pray together, but not simply for their own selfish concerns; they will pray for the people whom they have
grown to love at the mission outpost. Together, they will
discuss family sacrifice as they give up a trip to the beach
for spring break and instead provide an opportunity for
apartment kids to have a fun and productive time out of
school. As an added bonus, while engaged in their ministry,
they will work alongside surrogate grandparents, singles,
and childless adults.

We will also seek numerous mission ventures beyond
Off-Campus Ministries through which to connect the generations, such as Habitat for Humanity, mission trips, and
others. In addition to mission endeavors, we will provide
various intergenerational classes and family Bible study
opportunities.

One creative approach has been initiated informally by
some younger families in our church. Several fathers who
have six- or seven-year-old daughters have banded together. Their children attend different elementary schools, but
attend Sunday school together. In order to provide these
children an opportunity to get to know each other, the
fathers formed a sort of informal club. Dads and daughters
meet together weekly to work on crafts of various sorts.
Additionally, they take field trips to the zoo or a hands-on
museum or some other fun place, plus they go camping.
Together they talk about spiritual things as a natural part of
their common life, building values into the children as they
develop ever deeper bonds between themselves and the

other families. This is truly an example of a family of families on a spiritual journey.

(6) Recreation. We enjoy the luxury of owning a gymnasium as part of our facilities. This has been used to good effect for youth volleyball, adult basketball, and a hundred other activities. However, until now, we have offered little in the way of recreational opportunities for families. A church softball league is still a good activity to offer, but it is insufficient for our purposes. Rather, our task force will investigate a whole range of alternative recreational strategies: father and son baseball weekends; father and daughter softball where dad bats from the opposite side of the plate; family picnics complete with games; and a regular "family game night" with a wide range of active and interactive games. Children especially enjoy recreation, and so can their parents.

Additional Questions

The task force was asked to consider seven other items as it puts together its final plan:

(1) How do we ensure that our family ministry is specifically Christian? It is certainly conceivable that we could develop a family-friendly program that in fact has nothing to do with the Christian faith. We must somehow ensure that this ministry, like all others in the church, is designed to fulfill the basic mission of the church, to make disciples for Jesus Christ. Everyone in our society, including non-Christians and those antagonistic to the faith, at least purports to want a strong family, but ultimately we have nothing to offer apart from Christ. We must not allow ourselves to go down some side road, doing good, but missing God. This leads us to question two.

(2) What values underlie our family ministries? We speak about family values, but what specifically are those values? We must define exactly what we are attempting to instill in our community. We might be tempted to replace truly universal Christian values with patriotic Americanism or some other *-ism*. We must specifically detail the values we believe should underlie our ministry and then sift them through the Scriptures. Could a Christian in fourth-century Tibet or a believer in twenty-first-century Peru subscribe to the same values? If not, we may be off base.

(3) How do we get lay ownership? If this is only *my* vision, it will never blossom. In addition to the reasons cited above for excluding staff members from the task force, lay ownership will help ensure that the "Family Church" is the congregation's vision for our church rather than simply the staff's. It is a fine line that a leader walks between casting a vision and controlling it. The task force will develop its own strategies for transferring ownership to the church at large.

(4) What staff is needed? Eventually, we will need staff persons to manage this ministry. What kind of staff? What qualifications are necessary? Is ordination required, optional, or detrimental? Should we hire someone who is already a member of the congregation or shall we seek an outside expert? All of these questions must be answered at some point, though perhaps not all at the outset. Nevertheless, the issues must be brought to the forefront from the beginning.

(5) Can we "piecemeal it," or will that only inoculate us and ultimately undermine the effort? This is a crucial question related to how fully the ministry must be implemented at its beginning. Under at least one scenario, to

start small may ensure ultimate failure if the congregation grows bored with or sees nothing new in a little first-phase effort. On the other hand, it is difficult to launch into a full-blown program all at once. These two poles must be juxtaposed against one another as we decide how to launch our ministry.

(6) Should we set up a separate 501(c)3 corporation and go after foundation grants? It is altogether possible to petition any number of private foundations for grant funds to underwrite at least some of the components of the "Family Church" model. There is a great deal of interest in funding programs that help families, that bring meaning and hope to family life, that prevent or treat child abuse, and more. Obviously, there are potential risks to joining forces with outside entities. They may wish to control content or strategy or both, which could be detrimental to our main mission. However, theoretically, we should be able to uncover foundations that might find our proposals highly attractive. Indeed, if current trends continue, we may even be able to look for governmental (federal or state) support. To do so will require a measure of intentional effort, for the competition for funding is intense.

(7) What is the time line? All of the above will need to be fitted into a reasonable time line. This is where we finally put the plan into the concrete, answering the overarching question: "Who does what and when?"

Facing the Future

Where will God lead us? We simply do not know. Neither are we certain how we will get to the destination once it is revealed. Today we have inklings, and with that we will be content. For we do know that God is leading, and our God is more than able to show us the way. Our part is to open our lives to whatever visions God may place in our hearts, and then to open our minds for strategizing on just how to get there. We are a work in progress, a small part of the greater mosaic that is being fashioned by the master builder of the universe. We can count upon the God who has led the people of faith throughout the centuries, who no doubt will continue that work until its completion. This is God's eternal promise to us all.

Sample *TNT* Worksheet

APPENDIX

| Matthew 1 | January 1 |

 TO KNOW ...

Genealogies are not usually our favorite parts of the Bible, but they are important. They root the biblical record firmly in history. "These things" happened to real people somewhere in time.

Genealogies also show God's way of dealing with sinful humanity. For example, five women are listed as ancestors of Jesus in Matthew 1:

TAMAR (3),* who seduced her father-in-law, Judah, and by him bore her sons.

RAHAB (5), a harlot who barely escaped death by befriending the Hebrew spies at Jericho.

RUTH (5), a foreigner, a former pagan, who chose to follow her Hebrew mother-in-law, Naomi.

BATHSHEBA (6), an adulteress who married her husband's murderer.

MARY (16), a pregnant, unwed teenager. Although we know God's Spirit had overshadowed her, the rest of her world did not.

Of the five, which would we have chosen to be included in the forebears of the Christ? Yet God selected them all! God is indeed a redemptive God, who "saves to the uttermost."

TO DO...

1. How has God worked to bring good from my past sins?

2. What can I do to help redeem a past tragedy in my life?

*Numbers in parenthesis refer to verses in the same chapter of your reading.

If God is for us, who can be against us?
— St. Paul

Matthew 2　　　**January 2**

TO KNOW...

Wise men (probably astrologers) arrived in Jerusalem looking for the newborn King. They had seen unmistakable signs in the heavens that he was born. The priests and scribes told them that Micah 5:2 prophesied the Messiah would be born in Bethlehem. The *Child* (not baby) that they found was in a *house* (not a stable). The shepherds had long since departed. Jesus was perhaps as much as two years old when the wise men finally arrived (verse 16).

Matthew carefully shows how God was everpresent in the whole of Jesus' life, and especially at his birth. The wise men were warned not to report back to the insanely jealous King Herod. Joseph was then led to flee with his family into Egypt. They were directed to return only after the death of Herod, and then into Galilee rather than back to Bethlehem. The new ruler, Archelaus, was every bit as wicked and power hungry as his father. (His first act as king was to massacre 3,000 of his subjects.) God guided each step of the way so as to protect the newborn King and at the same time to fulfill prophecy.

TO DO...

1.　Wise men offered gold and other costly gifts to the Christ Child. What have I offered him?

2.　Where have I seen God's protecting hand in my life?

The Son of God became the Son of man that the children of men might become the children of God.　　**—St. Athanasius**

NOTES

1. The Explosive Power of *TNT*

1. Additional information about *TNT* may be received from the author at P.O. Box 551389, Dallas, TX 75355, or call toll-free at (800) 884-1155.

2. See Appendix for a sample worksheet.

3. Who Are the People in Your Neighborhood?

1. My thanks to Charles Lee Williamson, many years the Director of Missions for the Baptist General Convention of Texas, who developed this model. For additional insight on this issue, see Charles Lee Williamson, with Margaret McCommon Dempsey, *Growing Your Church in Seven Days* (Dallas: Creative Church Consultations, 1995).

2. See the author's Ph.D. dissertation, *Black and White Members and Ministers in The United Methodist Church: A Comparative Analysis,* 1991 (available through *Dissertation Abstracts*), for an analysis of the North Texas Annual Conference. In it, he found that both African American and White members are overwhelmingly middle- and upper-middle-class in education, income, and occupational category.

4. 9:44 and More

1. December 13, 1996, page 22F.

2. For additional insights on initiating change, see Lyle E. Schaller, *Strategies for Change* (Nashville: Abingdon Press, 1993).

3. Christian Copyright Licensing Inc., 6130 NE 78th Court, Suite C11, Portland, OR 97218. Phone: (800) 234-2446.

4. Willow Creek Association, P.O. Box 3188, Barrington, IL 60011. Phone: (847) 765-0070.

5. Outside the Four Walls

1. J. V. Thomas, *Investing in Eternity; The Indigenous Satellite Church Strategy; A Practical Guide to Multi-Church Planting* (1991). Available through the Baptist General Convention of Texas.

2. For additional information about the presuppositions and implications of off-campus ministries, see Lyle E. Schaller, *Innovations in Ministry* (Nashville: Abingdon Press, 1994).

3. I use the terms *she* and *her* advisedly. Because nationally more than 98 percent of apartment managers are female, I will refer to them throughout with feminine pronouns.

4. For additional help on dealing with apartment managers, see Barbara Oden (1992) *The "How To" Book for Starting Ministry & Congregations in Multihousing Communities* (for copies, write to 2060 N. Loop West, Suite #100, Houston, TX 77018).

5. Pamela and I are considering the possibility of hosting a "how-to" conference in the near future for other mainline churches who may wish to explore the off-campus model.

8. What Kind of Leader Am I?

1. For example, look at *Leadership Journal,* or read any of the many excellent books by Lyle Schaller, or check into the offerings of *Leadership Network.*

2. There is a rather large body of sociological literature on this subject. Perhaps the most famous work is Erving Goffman's landmark volume, *The Presentation of Self in Everyday Life* (Garden City, N.Y.: Doubleday, 1959).

3. The *Myers-Briggs Type Indicator* is an excellent resource for studying temperament. In order to access *Myers-Briggs,* see David Keirsey and Marilyn Bates, *Please Understand Me: Character and Temperament Types* (Del Mar, Cal.: Prometheus Nemesis Books, 1978). A brief introduction is provided by Thomas Moore, "Personality Tests Are Back," *Fortune,* March 30, 1987, pp. 83-87.

4. In *Stories for the Heart: When Your Soul Needs More than Chicken Soup,* Alice Gray (Sisters, Ore.: Multnomah Books, 1996), p. 225.

5. "Geech," by Jerry Bittle, Universal Press Syndicate, 1997.

9. Assembling a "Dream Team" of Your Own

1. Kennon Callahan, *Twelve Keys to an Effective Church* (San Francisco: Harper & Row, 1983).

10. Second Thoughts

1. See 2 Corinthians 12:9.